THE AVENGERS
FACE THEIR
DARK SIDES

Other Works by Valerie Estelle Frankel

Henry Potty and the Pet Rock: A Harry Potter Parody
Henry Potty and the Deathly Paper Shortage: A Harry Potter Parody
Buffy and the Heroine's Journey
From Girl to Goddess: The Heroine's Journey in Myth and Legend
Katniss the Cattail: The Unauthorized Guide to Name and Symbols in The Hunger Games
The Many Faces of Katniss Everdeen: Exploring the Heroine of The Hunger Games
Harry Potter, Still Recruiting: A Look at Harry Potter Fandom
Teaching with Harry Potter
An Unexpected Parody: The Spoof of The Hobbit Movie
Teaching with Harry Potter
Myths and Motifs in The Mortal Instruments
Winning the Game of Thrones: The Host of Characters & their Agendas
Winter is Coming: Symbols, Portents, and Hidden Meanings in A Game of Thrones
Bloodsuckers on the Bayou: The Myths, Symbols, and Tales Behind HBO's True Blood
The Girl's Guide to the Heroine's Journey
Choosing to be Insurgent or Allegiant: Symbols, Themes & Analysis of the Divergent Trilogy
Doctor Who and the Hero's Journey: The Doctor and Companions as Chosen Ones
Doctor Who: The What Where and How
Sherlock: Every Canon Reference You May Have Missed in BBC's Series 1-3
Symbols in Game of Thrones
How Game of Thrones Will End
Joss Whedon's Names
Pop Culture in the Whedonverse
Women in Game of Thrones: Power, Conformity, and Resistance
History, Homages and the Highlands: An Outlander Guide
The Catch-Up Guide to Doctor Who
Remember All Their Faces: A Deeper Look at Character, Gender and the Prison World of Orange Is The New Black
Everything I Learned in Life I Know from Joss Whedon
Empowered: The Symbolism, Feminism, and Superheroism of Wonder Woman

THE AVENGERS FACE THEIR DARK SIDES

Mastering the Myth-Making
behind the Marvel
Superheroes

Valerie Estelle Frankel

This book is an unauthorized guide and commentary on the Marvel films and their associated comics. None of the individuals or companies associated with the comics, films, television shows or any merchandise based on this series has in any way sponsored, approved, endorsed, or authorized this book.

ISBN-13: 978-0692432457 (LitCrit Press)
ISBN-10: 0692432450

Contents

THE AVENGERS FACE THEIR DARK SIDES

Introduction: The Myth of Superheroes from Silver Age to Modern Age

Americans have always needed superheroes, or their ancestors, mythology and epic. Superheroes represent a distinctly American form of storytelling that nonetheless builds on these traditions. The American monomyth, according to Robert Jewett and John Shelton Lawrence, has the following steps:

1. A community is threatened.
2. A selfless hero emerges
3. The hero renounces temptation
4. The hero wins a victory (through superheroism)
5. The hero restores harmony to the community
6. The hero recedes into obscurity (Duncan and Smith 232)

The pattern listed emphasizes the hero's personal struggle as temptation is a factor. And yet, the deepest, most compelling superhero stories offer something more. Those superhero stories bring in the classic monomyth – Joseph Campbell's hero's journey.

In this classic quest, the hero quests, often on behalf of his community, and battles a dark force. Yet this enemy is most threatening because it represents the buried part of the hero – all the brutal, selfish and tyrannical longings he pushes away in order to become a paragon. Superman faces Bizarro, Thor battles Loki. At the same time, the buried impulses, known in Jungian psychology as the Shadow, have much to offer – strength and insight as a more experienced way of seeing the world. Thus each shadow encounter has the potential for enormous growth:

For the individual, one of the major tasks in the process of psychological development is to recognize, acknowledge, and

accept those rejected aspects of the self (the shadow). The process of integration through acknowledging and accepting the shadow aspects of our personalities gives us depth and access to a greater range of expression. Oftentimes the shadow will hold hitherto unknown powers and capabilities. (Von Franz 170-171)

The true victory is over the enemy and simultaneously over the self – to learn from the dark power within, acknowledge it, yet not be consumed by it. These heroic stories have always appealed to readers, though for many years comic books were dismissed as easy stories for children despite their mythic strength. In fact, the hero's journey is often a metaphor for adulthood as one understands the self better through this encounter and is thus prepared for adult responsibility. "It is no accident that superhero stories appeal most to those who are in the midst of change themselves. Pubescents and early adolescents, whose bodies are changing, were the audience of the first superhero comics" (Parker 125).

As Stan Lee explains, when he started at Marvel, or rather, Timely Comics, "Comics were so – I won't say hated – but were so disrespected in those days, most parents didn't even want their kids to read comics. If ever anybody over the age of twelve or thirteen was seen with a comic you'd think there was something wrong with him, and people just had no respect at all for comics" ("Afterward"). Since he planned to write the great American novel, he reserved his real name, Stanley Lieber, for that and wrote comics as Stan Lee. Lee had been working at Timely since he was seventeen, working his way up from office boy. Now he was growing bored and frustrated, though his monster comics were selling well. His wife advised him to write his dream project before he left.

Around this time, Timely's publisher, Martin Goodman, had a legendary golf game with National Comics publisher Jack Liebowitz, where Liebowitz boasted about how well the new Justice League of America comic was selling. After the game, Goodman called Lee and asked him to work on a superhero team comic book.

Stan Lee went back to first principles. In his universe, heroes needed reasons, motivations. "While the Golden Age heroes were reactive, always coming to save the day from supervillains in plot driven stories, silver age heroes were more contemplative. Their heroism was often motivated by pain or other emotional hangups, and they did a great deal of soul-searching while in their suits" (Duncan and Smith 232). Famed comic book writer Grant Morrison says:

> Unlike the DC heroes, with their totemistic weaknesses to wood or fire (or the color yellow, as in the case of the new Schwartz version of Green Lantern), every Marvel hero had to have a psychological Achilles' heel. If they didn't harbor a deadly personal secret capable of destroying careers and marriages, they weren't good Marvel heroes. And they fought constantly. Superheroes had battled against injustice in the 1930s and fought Hitler in the 1940s, while the 1950s superheroes had battled with monsters and aliens. The Marvel heroes of the 1960s fought one another between epic clashes with memorably operatic villains such as Doctor Doom, Magneto, Galactus, Doctor Octopus, and the Green Goblin, all of whom had personalities and extra dimensions that elevated them beyond the traditional despots, hoodlums, and madmen (100)

As the supervillains developed, they became each superhero's nemesis and shadow – a force that used the opposite powers of the hero to wreak havoc and destruction. The hero can learn from this encounter to grow as a person. "The shadow usually contains values that are needed by consciousness, but that exist in a form that makes it difficult to integrate them into one's life" (Von Franz 178). Stan Lee discarded costumed superheroes with secret identities and flimsy love triangles between hero, naïve girlfriend, and his secret identity. He created the Fantastic Four, a family team who squabbled and bickered. They wore astronaut jumpsuits and proclaimed their identities to the world. Further, Sue, the hero's fiancée had her own set of superpowers. All the heroes were driven by their hangups and complications. Few Marvel characters automatically succumb to fire or kryptonite. "Their limitations are rooted in their own personalities: pride (Thor), brashness (Human Torch), addictive personality (Iron Man), self-doubt (Spider-Man), and even some instances of self-loathing (Hulk)" (Duncan and Smith 227). More heroes followed: The raging Hulk, billionaire genius Iron Man, Angst-filled teen Spider Man, Thor, the X-Men, the Avengers. The characters, unusually, showed up in each other's stories with great frequency, emphasizing their shared universe.

Marvel was breaking the mold in other ways—stories were multi-issue, often with complex subplots. The Marvel Method emerged, with the script created after the penciled art rather than before. Editorial boxes chatted with fans, including them with winks and nods. Writers and artists all took friendly nicknames. The superheroes fought monsters in the immediate New York, rather than distant "Gotham" or "Metropolis." "The Fantastic Four bickered when stressed, and Spider-Man worried about making ends meet, introducing a more human or flawed element to the superhero genre which had often been populated by paragons of humanity's ideals" (Darowski 201).

Fast forwarding to recent times, after 9/11, a superhero renaissance arrived as people were desperate to feel in control. Indeed, "since the year 2000, the United States has seen 70 live action and 41 animated superhero movies, whereas the previous 50 years produced less than half of this total" (Coyne, Linder, Rasmussen, Nelson and Collier 417). Everyone was desperate to heal the wounded "feelings of helplessness and terror that Americans experienced in the days and years following the [9/11] attack" (Hagley and Harrison 120).

Morrison explains that post-9/11, "With no way to control the growing unreality of the wider world, writers and artists attempted to tame it in fiction that became more and more 'grounded,' down-to-earth, and rooted in the self-consciously plausible. And so was born *Ultimate Marvel*" (348). The series was set in a realistic world with George W. Bush, Samuel L. Jackson, and Freddy Prinze Jr. Publicity and media spin were central. Characters debated the US's warmongering policies, though even the Greenpeace-loving Thor joined up when danger threatened – everyone, liberal or conservative – was Team America in the end. And they kicked the enemy's butts. Meanwhile, Pym mused, "I never asked for Homeland Security or Guantanamo Bay or this big preemptive strike they made us do on a third world country" (*Gods and Monsters*).

"Marvel stepped into the post-9/11 breach with global-political thrillers that acknowledged contemporary events without dwelling on them" (348). The image appeared of "global law enforcement in a posttraumatic world" (348), though problems appeared as well as triumphs. The writer Brian Bendis "influenced by playwright David Mamet rather than Stan Lee…made alarmingly convincing dialogue the focus of his style" (348). There were constant pop culture references mixed into the snappy dialogue, reminding readers that the characters were just like them. Anticipating the films, the comics riffed a great deal on adaptation, as publicist Betty Ross insists, "The difference between us and Hollywood, General, as that I'm going to make the Ultimates *really* famous" (*Super – Human*). Brad Pitt signs up to play Captain America and the team debate who should play them onscreen.

> Life became art became life when Nick Fury, agent of S.H.I.E.L.D., was recast in the image of Samuel L. Jackson, following a scene in *The Ultimates* in which the character of Fury himself had actually suggested Jackson as the ideal actor to play him, in a Mobius-loop of such self-referential, cross-dimensional complexity, my powers of description fail me. The circuit ws closed and the current sparked from page to screen to life when comics fan Samuel L. Jackson was asked to play Ultimate Nick Fury in Iron Man (Morrison 349)

"*The Ultimates* gave comic readers a much more realistic treatment of Captain America a hero who represented the lost world of traditional patriotic values, an old hero for a new age. The terrorist attacks of 9/11 reawakened American patriotism, which had been deeply problematized since Vietnam" (Murray, *Champions of the Oppressed* 253). The 9/11 attacks gave Captain America a new purpose in a world in which patriotism was no longer silly. *The Ultimates* welcomed Captain America to the twenty-first century with a handshake from President Bush, who asked Captain America if he found the twenty-first century "cool or uncool?" Cap replied, "Definitely cool." He was a welcome burst of light as he told troops, "Your country needs you," and yelled, "You think this letter on my head stands for France?" when asked to surrender, a moment that spurred American patriotism (*Homeland Security*). "His bluster gave heart to an injured nation" (Morrison 349).

> The Promethean age had been announced; the time of men as gods who bore fire in the palms of their hands had come. And with that recognition of the superhero's Promethean dimension came the acknowledgment of punishment, Fall, retribution, and guilt—themes that would resonate through the experience of a very unusual generation of children. From now on, having superpowers would come at the very least

with great responsibility and, at worst, would be regarded as a horrific curse. (Morrison 89)

Grant Morrison suggests that as "we tell our children they're trapped like rats on a doomed, bankrupts, gangster-haunted planet with dwindling resources, with nothing to look forward to but rising seas levels and immanent mass extinctions," (xvii) we all need superheroes to give us hope, especially now. "Superhero stories speak loudly and boldly to our greatest fears, deepest longings, and highest aspirations. They're not afraid to be hopeful, not embarrassed to be optimistic, and utterly fearless in the dark" (xvii).

In the wake of these new, more realistic comics and their world-examining themes, Marvel executives resolved to make their own films the way they as fans wanted to see them done. The characters would be real people, not silly caricatures, and they would face their own flaws through the superpowers and epic battles. They would share Stan Lee's vision, and also his shared universe concept. With *Spider-Man*, *Fantastic Four*, and *X-Men* contracted away, another set of Marvel heroes stepped up:

> **Five years ago, Marvel executives developed a comprehensive plan involving four superheroes to culminate with one "uber" movie, says Marvel's Paul Gitter. "We took the superheroes — Iron Man, Captain America, Thor, and Hulk — that we felt were the most relatable, relevant, and aspirational to build into one package. Every Marvel movie since 2008 was created with the full intention of this super franchise." (Faw)**

Today, the MCU is not an old-school superhero series, but a new one, reflecting *Ultimate Marvel*, especially in the costumes, attitudes, and scenarios.

"With new tellers and half a century to work with, superhero origin stories are often rebooted. The retellings are expected to add a new aspect to the character, color him with the new creative team's style, and preserve continuity as much as possible" (Reynolds 48). The MCU reboots all its characters, ignoring the *Daredevil* film, or even the *Hulk* film from only a few years before, to tell its stories from the beginning. Despite this, the writers make a serious effort to incorporate pieces of the classic origin stories – *The Avengers*, for instance, blends the 1960s first comic's plot – Loki plans to unleash the Hulk on the Avengers, giving them a common enemy, with the Chitauri invasion of *The Ultimates*. Hulk's director Louis Lettier notes that President of Marvel Kevin Feige said, "I trust fans more than I trust technicians. I want people that will give it their all and really have a passion for the material." Thus many little nods like this appear. Though Edward Norton doesn't wear purple pants, Betty Ross buys him a set in a quick wink for fans. In fact, easter eggs like this one abound in the films, offering little waves from creators to fans, much like the Stan Lee cameos, a way of rewarding those who are fans of the entire Marvel and MCU universes and have shown up for more than to watch Hulk smash.

This book likewise rewards the deeper watchers and thinkers. There's a catalog of easter eggs at book's end, and summaries of many of the origin stories, but mostly this book examines the heroes and their journeys through psychological symbolism. Why does Fury tell playboy Tony he needs to fix his heart before he becomes an Avenger and why must he go into the basement, home of the subconscious to do so (let alone tear it down!)? Does everyone have a monster within them like the Hulk? Who is Black Widow psychologically, and does she even know? Why is Peter Quill so hung up on his mother and how does her image help him to grow? Why is Daredevil the only MCU character to keep his secret identity and what does this mean for him? Exploring all these questions, this book probes the deeper meaning of these tales and reveals why they mean so much to us – they're all metaphors for the human condition.

THE AVENGERS FACE THEIR DARK SIDES

The MCU Films

Facing the Father: Iron Man

Back in 1963, Stan had an idea for a superhero who was also a successful businessman, a jet-setting Howard Hughes type. But Stan's rich protagonist needed a reason to go out in a costume and risk his life fighting bad guys. Once more, Lee put it all together. As he recounts in *Son of Origins of Marvel Comics*, "What if our hero had an injured heart – a heart that required him to wear some sort of metal device to keep it beating? The metal device could be the basic element in an entire suit of armor which could both power him and conceal his identity. I loved it. It had the right ring to it. I knew it would work." (Ryall and Tipton)

"It was Iron Man—a B-list Marvel star—who gave notice of a new kind of superhero film, one that could reach a bigger audience than ever before" (Morrison 378). Morrison adds that "Billionaire tech genius Stark represented the twenty-first-century model of success in an America whose wartime symbol Captain America was an essentially outmoded picture of self-reliant rugged individualism, a pioneer spirit no longer welcome in a globally connected world" (Morrison 353). But Tony offers hot new gadgets as he scribbles in the air and his computers bring to life all his ideas.

Living in a world of toys, sports cars, and intelligent robots, he creates twenty-first century "smarter weapons, advanced robotics, satellite targeting," as the movie tells. His greatest tool is math, which for him is always right. As he resolves to invent clean, renewable energy and lives in a world controlled by JARVIS, he's a superhero of tech and genius, not just heart. As such, he's all brilliance, a hero of the modern age in which Bill Gates or Steve

Jobs can rule the world. "The enduring appeal of Iron Man owes a great deal to how Tony Stark personifies the spectacular promise of technology to turn our dreams into reality, a promise that has stoked a fire in the bellies of countless men and women in the modern era, not only in preadolescent boys with airborne imaginations" (Dunn, Kindle Locations 2442-2444).

What's more, he's Robert Downey Jr., who's described playing Tony Stark as playing himself, only with better toys.

> No one could have summoned to life the Tony Stark of *The Ultimates* with the flair and insight that he brought to the role. Iron Man was the perfect breakthrough superhero for the blankly aspirational first decade of the twenty-first century. He was the millionaire man-and-machine cyborg we were all becoming, grafted to our phones and VDUs, our poker faces like locked and polished doors. (Morrison 378)

The first movie offers something deeper, dealing with father-images and choosing an adult identity. Tony's entire career has been fashioned after his father's and "uncle's" expectations – he invents weapons because they did and because he wants to further his father's goal of weapons as a deterrent. He spends the rest of his time on pleasure – drinking, gambling, and having fun. A lighthearted playboy, Tony rationalizes everything and never takes responsibility. Rhodey tells him, "You don't respect yourself, so I know you don't respect me." As Tony assures the woman interviewing him from *Vanity Fair*:

> Tony Stark: Well, Ms. Brown, it's an imperfect world, but it's the only one we've got. I guarantee you, the day weapons are no longer needed to keep the peace, I'll start making bricks and beams for baby hospitals.
> Interviewer: Rehearse that much?
> Tony Stark: Every night in front of the mirror before bedtime.

Of course, as Jungian psychologist Clarissa Pinkola Estés warns: "Overkill through excesses, or excessive behaviors, is acted out by women [or men] who are famished for a life that has meaning and makes sense for them" (248). A change is coming for the superficial hero.

"In the first stage of this kind of adventure, the hero leaves the realm of the familiar, over which he has some measure of control, and comes to a threshold" (Campbell 146). In the kidnappers' cave, Tony sees for the first time what he's become. "I guess you have everything…and nothing," smirks his rescuer Yinsen, a genius who's been resisting his captors for the sake of his family. The mentor is an essential figure from the Otherworld, one who awakens hidden gifts in the hero. "For those who have not refused the call, the first encounter of the hero-journey is with a protective figure (often a little old crone or old man) who provides the adventurer with amulets against the dragon forces he is about to pass" (Campbell 69). As Yinsen reassures the traumatized hero, he also challenges him ("Is this how the great Tony Stark goes out?"). Thus Tony resolves to create something all his own, a weapon to save himself and fight the evil he's seen in his first real combat.

In the post-9/11 universe of the MCU, Tony begins his first adventure fighting vaguely Middle Eastern terrorists in the desert. The men however have many nationalities, as Yinsen says, "They speak Arabic, Urdu, Dari, Pashto, Mongolian, Farsi, Russian." All this signals American self-determination against worldwide violence. This is an update from his original origins, though much in the same spirit:

> More than any of the other Marvel comics of the era, Iron Man was caught up in the fervor of Cold War America — Iron Man represented the power of American technology and scientific know-how that would quash those backwards Commies. Iron Man's Silver Age rogues' gallery tells the tale, boasting such baddies as the Soviet armored doppelgänger the Crimson Dynamo, the Red Chinese warlord the Mandarin (sporting ten super-powered rings, one for each finger), the Soviet spy known as the Black Widow (who would later defect to the U.S. and become Iron Man's teammate), and another Russian armored-type, Titanium Man. (Ryall and Tipton)

Iron Man premiered in *Tales of Suspense* #39 (March 1963). While Tony Stark, a millionaire industrialist, is testing his new "transistor-powered" mortar cannons, in Vietnam, he accidentally triggers a mine. Near death, with shrapnel advancing on his heart, he is captured by the Viet Cong despot Wong-Chu, "the red guerrilla tyrant" of South Vietnam.

Wong Chu forces him to build a superweapon, but Tony confides in a fellow prisoner, Professor Yinsen, "once the greatest physicist of them all." The pair build an Iron Man suit to keep

Tony's heart beating and allow his escape, but Yinsen sacrifices himself to allow Tony a chance to survive. Tony, now in his charged armor with many gadgets, destroys Wong-Chu and his base, blowing up the guerrilla's ammo dump. "Although he's sentenced to virtual life imprisonment in his invincible suit of armor, Stark draws strength from his infirmity – the trademark of a classic Marvel superhero" (Ridout 4). He also realizes he can survive with only the chest plate, though he keeps his distance from everyone, rather than reveal his secret identity.

> ... Dubbing his new creation Iron Man, Stan turned over the plot to his brother Larry Lieber, who the previous year had conceptualized Stan's notion, to provide the script. As for the art, Don Heck provided the pencils, as he would for many of the succeeding Iron Man adventures. Jack Kirby, meanwhile, contributed the design of the original Iron Man armor, as well as the cover for the debut appearance. (Ryall and Tipton)

Thus the legend was born.

Upon returning home in the film, Tony insists he'll no longer make weapons after seeing "the very Americans" he was trying to protect torn up by them. "No one can go through an experience at the edge of death without being changed in some way," warns hero-myth scholar Christopher Vogler (30). In Tony's case, he's learned responsibility. Similarly in *The Ultimates* comics, he ponders, "I guess I just hit a point in my life when I wondered what things could be like if all the billionaires and government spooks tried to *save* the world instead of bleeding it dry" (*Super-Human*). He later reveals in the comic that he has a brain tumor and wants to do good with his life instead of endlessly acquiring useless treasures.

Film Tony follows his announcement by going a step further, atoning for his life of indulgence by creating the new Iron Man suit—his technology will no longer injure people but save them. Further, his immense fortune won't go into luxuries and toys but a device that makes Tony Stark into a hero. He goes out and risks his life, he takes bumps and bruises in training, and he begins to reject the lustful luxuries around him, smashing a few sports cars in practice and ignoring parties to work in his machine shop. As Tony reflects in "Why Must There Be an Iron Man?" (*Iron Man* #47), "Sometimes I'm out in a crowd and I hear somebody's scornful whisper: 'Munitions Maker!' And I find myself pondering every action I ever made. But maybe that's all to the good."

He begins the film emphasizing that the biggest most powerful weapon was "how Dad did it," but after his ordeal, he's changed, especially in his paternal legacy. As he muses at the press conference:

> I never got to say goodbye to Dad. I never got to say goodbye to my father. There's questions that I would have asked him. I would have asked him how he felt about what this company did. If he was conflicted, if he ever had doubts. Or maybe he was every inch the man we all remember from the newsreels.

Back home, he crafts a better heart for himself, mirroring his inner transformation. Pepper enshrines the old one in glass, with the caption that it's proof Tony has a heart, but the proof isn't needed, as children on the news cry that a masked hero saved their lives. "What could have been post-traumatic stress disorder (PTSD) turns into positive and becomes 'post-traumatic *strength* disorder'" Sharon Packer notes of the character in *Superheroes and Superegos: Analyzing the Minds behind the Masks* (39).

The armor of course *is* the film, and more, is the character. "We've had artists working on it for nearly a year now," Feige said, "designing what I believe is the single most successful translation of a character from comics to the big screen, and the best version of the suit that has ever existed" ("Feige on Silver Surfer"). Though the Iron Man suit is unique, Stark uses it to do something his father and uncle have never done—fight villains personally. He becomes an ally of the military, the ultimate patriarchy, but resists joining it. St least superficially, he remains loyal to his uncle, keeping the company alive but reprioritizing until his need for heroism takes precedence. As one of Tony's female companions once described his *Iron Man* alter ego in the comics, "he has a heart of gold and an appearance to match his golden deeds" (*Tales of Suspense* #40).

Meanwhile, Stane pressures him to consider big business and war profiteering before conscience. As well as the voice of Tony's forceful surrogate father, he's also the villainous corporate CEO with his smart black suit and tie, the default big, bad wolf of eighties comics. "Listen to me, Tony. We're a team. Do you understand? There's nothing we can't do if we stick together, like your father and I," Stane tells him, putting on the family pressure.

> Stane [is] a sort of dark doppelganger of Tony. Like Tony, he's a powerful tycoon and weapons mogul, although his corporate intrigues are not in the service of old-fashioned chivalric virtues such as generosity but rather the newfangled capitalist virtue of greed instead. Suddenly, Tony's archenemy is ... a ruthless domestic capitalist who ends up possessing much of Tony's technology and none of his ideals. (Dunn, Kindle Locations 2640-2643).

By the movie's end, the uncle is mimicking Tony, trying to live up to his ideal through his own Ironmonger suit. However, his incomplete understanding of it leads to his demise. As Tony explains, "I am Iron Man." The uncle is not—he has the soul of an entrepreneur, not an inventor or freedom fighter.

In the comics, Obadiah Stane is not an adoptive father, but a rival businessman who acquires Stark Industries. He and Stark are also romantic rivals. Stane, who wishes to defeat and humiliate his enemy as crushingly as Lex Luthor defeats Superman, finds one of Tony's notebooks and begins the Ironmonger project. "Its possibilities are endless. I can sell it to any nation on earth for more money than anyone has ever *dreamt* of possessing," he cackles. The pair each don their armor in similarly framed scenes and face off, Stane in blue and Stark in a new red and silver suit (*Iron Man* #200). Stane holds Stark's friend hostage and even threatens to crush a baby, emphasizing his brutal ruthlessness. Stark of course manages to save everyone.

As with the film, Stark's research provides Stane with his massive new toy. Both times Stark takes advantage of a creator's tools – knowing his product far better than the man who only copies it. On the show, he flies so high that the armor freezes and in the comic, the armor halts because Stane is controlling it by external computer – something the armor was programmed to resist. The inventor will always triumph over the businessman.

In the film, he's called a visionary and genius. As the film introduces him, "Even from an early age, the son of legendary weapons developer Howard Stark quickly stole the spotlight with his brilliant and unique mind. At age four, he built his first circuit board. At age six, his first engine. And at seventeen, he graduated *summa cum laude* from MIT."

> Unlike, say, Reed Richards of the Fantastic Four, Tony wasn't
> simply someone who happened to be a superhero in addition
> to being a hotshot engineer. He was a superhero because of
> those jet boots and the enviable power they gave him, which
> is to say that it was his extraordinary engineering prowess
> that allowed him to make himself super, without having to wait
> around for gamma rays or a radioactive spider bite.... In
> principle, anyone could be Iron Man (Dunn, Kindle Locations
> 2428-2431)

While the first armor of the comics, like in the film, was bulky and grey, by Stark's next appearance in *Tales of Suspense* #40, it was more streamlined and could be folded into a briefcase. Over the years, the armor underwent many changes, from shape and color to the gadgets – from roller skates to repulsor beams. One of the plotters of *Iron Man*, David Michelinie, notes, "Technology certainly is not going to stand still, and Tony Stark, as a driven individual, is constantly expanding the frontiers of science" (qtd. in Ridout 7). Iron Man's tech includes repulsor rays, missile launchers, pulse beams, and flamethrowers as well as the jet boots. However, all the toys conceal a terribly vulnerable human being.

> Iron Man reminded us that our man-machine future was more
> than a simple triumph of soulless technology but involved an
> exchange, an eroticization and softening of metal's contours.
> Iron Man was no robot, as he may have appeared at first; the
> impenetrable armor concealed a soft center and those melting
> puppy dog eyes. The man of metal had a shattered heart of
> shrapnel. Tony Stark became the tender center, the wounded
> soul in the military machine that helped to sell a war and
> humanize its warriors. (Morrison 379)

Indeed, it's the character's caring and humanity under the snark as he's increasingly disillusioned, like a child without Santa, that truly makes fans care. Stan Lee recalls, "We later learned that, of all our Super Heroes, Iron Man got the most fan mail from females." True, he was a playboy millionaire, but Lee believed that it was also because "he had that weak heart and was a tragic figure" (Mangels 8). Along with the vulnerability came honor and an old-fashioned heroism.

The appeal of Iron Man owes just as much to the way his gleaming golden armor bathes him in the glory of a mythical past, a romantic world of medieval knights-errant, often graced with superhuman abilities, invincible in battle against an endless succession of menaces that threaten the peace of their kingdoms. (Dunn, Kindle Locations 2448-2453)

Stan Lee's account of how he first came up with the inspiration for Iron Man ties into the oldest traditions of chivalry as well as the newest of technological progress:

I thought, Well, what if a guy had a suit of armor, but it was a modern suit of armor—not like years ago in the days of King Arthur—and what if that suit of armor made him as strong as any Super Hero? I wasn't thinking robot at all; I was thinking armor, a man wearing twentieth century armor that would give him great power. (qtd. in Mangels 4)

Superheroes have a great deal of chivalry and nod to an older era of black and white morality with good guys fighting bad guys with mythic strength. Those telling the legends often understand this. During the 2012 *Believe* story arc, a group of new superheroes reinforce this. Naming themselves for Arthurian characters, they challenge Tony to a duel. They call him "the Grail Knight. He who is destined to retrieve the Grail and in doing so, understand ultimate truth." Tony admits he is, beats them, and reclaims their "Grail," Extremis. In the film, he realizes he has a duty to defend the helpless, as he has the power and privilege they lack.

Through the film, Tony grows up in other ways – his charm transfers from the many women he momentarily admires to Pepper as he seeks a more mature and mutual relationship. In the course of the tale, Tony asks Pepper to fix his heart (literally), adding, "You're the most capable, qualified, trustworthy person I've ever met. You're gonna do great," when she balks at the task. As she becomes his Iron Man confidante, a force of support and constancy as well as romance, she's indeed the right choice. Jungian psychologists believe that by falling in love and finding a person to complete us, we're really struggling to connect with lost and buried parts of ourselves. "Some people seem to discover their inner opposite *through* relationship, while others must abandon idolatrous levels of relating and turn directly inward" (DeBus 56). Superheroes with their terribly symbolic stories generally fall into the former category, and Tony is no exception – Pepper connects him to duty and responsibility, unlike the frivolous party girls of his past.

The metaphor stretches further as Stane tears out Tony's shining new superhero heart to power his own evil machine. Tony must take refuge with his Mark One heart, the heart of an ordinary inventor trapped in a cave, desperate to survive. This is not as powerful, but he manages to save the day with it nonetheless, all thanks to Pepper and her faith in him. Her faith saves him, as she preserves his first arc reactor unit as "Proof that Tony Stark Has a Heart" and he uses it to rescue himself.

On the hero's journey, Tony journeys into the realm of death "which is a well-known symbol of the unconscious with its unknown possibilities" (Von Franz 170). First comes the terrorists' cave, then a return to their lair. As the film's news show describes it:

> The 15-mile hike to the outskirts of Gulmira can only be described as a descent into hell, into a modern day Heart of Darkness. Simple farmers and herders from peaceful villages have been driven from their homes, displaced from their lands by warlords emboldened by a new-found power. Villagers have been forced to take shelter in whatever crude dwellings they can find in the ruins of other villages, or here in the remnants of an old Soviet smelting plant. Recent violence has been attributed to a group of foreign fighters referred to by locals as the Ten Rings. As you can see, these men are heavily armed and on a mission. A mission that could prove fatal to anyone who stands in their way.

As he goes there and rescues innocents, he transforms into a true superhero at last. The third journey into the underworld comes at the climax, when Pepper tracks Stane to his machine shop. The staging is gothic, with weird blue lights and smoke emanating spookily from the darkness, then suddenly, a pair of lit up eyes. As Stand looms over Pepper, gargantuan sized, and threatens to kill her, Tony arrives like a knight in shining armor to rescue his lady. Stane of course is the superhuman monster, hulking over the smaller hero. Meanwhile, Stane taunts Tony about making his father proud at last. Stane is a giant, older, corporate, and more experienced – the face of the patriarchy in every way.

Jungian writer Murray Stein compares the father-son battle to

Kronos and Zeus of Greek myth – "Under Kronos [the father-tyrant] consciousness is finely tuned to the prevailing values and attitudes of an outer collective" (77). Indeed, Stane appears to care most for "the board" and financial success. This father figure "is threatened by stirrings in the unconscious, by 'infantile' impulses, 'crazy' thoughts, 'childish' reactions" (77). This of course is creative, immature Tony. As with Kronos, Stane decides to murder this voice of creativity and change. As Stane gloats, by trying to make peace, he has invented the greatest weapon of all. As Tony battles him, he's battling the expectations of others, his out-of-control company, and of course, his substitute father.

> The earliest Iron Man comics were bursting with optimism about how a courageous and well-intentioned hero like Tony Stark, armed with cutting-edge technology, could vanquish the many foes of freedom in the world. But by the mid-eighties, it had become clear to Tony that he had unleashed forces he couldn't control. Unable to prevent the dissemination of his Iron Man armor designs to villains like Spymaster and Obadiah Stane (Iron Monger), Tony faced the sickening realization that the very technologies he designed to make the world safer were actually being used to put it at graver risk than it ever would have been without them. (Dunn, Kindle Locations 2635-2640).

Pepper, the one who cares for Tony's heart, gets a new mission – to take the industrial size arc reactor – a superheroic-sized heart in truth—and use its power to destroy the monster. The power of Tony's heart, commanded by Tony and wielded by Pepper, destroys the monster forever.

Battling the Shadow: Iron Man 2

Please, it's not about me. It's not about you. It's not even about us. It's about legacy. It's about what we choose to leave behind for future generations. And that's why for the next year and for the first time since 1974, the best and brightest men and women of nations and corporations the world over will pool their resources, share their collective vision, to leave behind a brighter future.

Tony's ego, shown as he makes the ultimate Iron Man entrance at the Stark Expo and the inspiring speech above, is one of his flaws, but it's not his greatest enemy. For though Tony pledges himself to idealism, determined to save innocents and use the Iron Man suit as a nuclear deterrent, others feel differently. Worse yet, though he's holding an enormous ego trip of an expo to mirror his father's Stark Expo of 1974, he doesn't truly believe in his father's legacy or his own. For Tony is dying, and as he tries to create a perfect image for the world to admire, cracks are beginning to appear.

In Jungian psychology, the shadow is all we bury deep within, allowing only the qualities we like to show. Tony Stark wants to appear responsible; he conceals his bratty side. He wants to appear controlled; he conceals his anger. The shadow reveals qualities the hero can see in other people but not in himself – "such things as egotism, mental laziness, and sloppiness; unreal fantasies, schemes, and plots; carelessness and cowardice; inordinate love of money and possessions – in short all the little sins about which he might have previously [ignored in himself]" (Von Franz 174). In fact, the

Iron Man suit allows Tony to conceal any number of flaws and appear the perfect hero, red and gleaming, face impassive and fearless. He insists, "I am Iron Man. The suit and I are one. To turn over the Iron Man suit would be to turn over myself" but he's losing conviction.

Underneath, his heart is shattering, breaking down under the strain. While this is literally true in the film, it's echoed by the metaphoric heartache as Tony can't handle a relationship with Pepper, a full time job managing his own and his uncle's job at Stark Industries, and his Iron Man persona as well. "Forming our personalities and committing our psychological energy to developing our personal lives through skills, work and relationships limits our access to the unconscious with its creative spiritual, and disorganizing influences" (DeBus 57). This is especially true for Tony, who's flung himself into partying to avoid his pressing need. His childish, selfish side, outgrown in the first movie has been suppressed too long under showmanship, public appearance, and duty. It's ready to break free.

Justin Hammer appears, a real life foe for Tony but also a physical embodiment of his buried shadow. "Whether the shadow becomes our friend or enemy depends largely upon ourselves … in fact, he is exactly like any human being with whom one has to get along" (Von Franz 182). Justin and Tony compete at every opportunity, as each sees the rejected part of himself in the flesh: Tony's selfishness, Justin's duty. Justin Hammer is just the opportunist Tony has always refused to be, eager to profit off his weapons. He reflects the childish selfishness that Stark pretends to on the surface as a shallow playboy, though as he proves in the Iron Man suit, his morality runs deeper. Justin Hammer, however, is all surface with nothing below. Tony's legacy is the Iron Man suit and the unlimited power that supplies it; Justin's is a smart missile "capable of reducing the population of any standing structure to zero," which he calls "the ex-wife." Interestingly, the device doesn't work—it is indeed all fraud and surface, just like him.

Unlike Tony, the creative force, Justin Hammer only pretends to invent—he takes credit for Tony's Iron Man prototype and Ivan's drones. When Tony takes over the military's television screens, Justin can manage nothing more than pulling the plug in response. Though he dances and makes an entrance at the Expo—presumably because that's what he believes a media icon does—his unoriginal, untalented dance is a reflection of him, just as Tony's multimillion dollar glitzy, over-the-top joyous entrance reflects his own personality.

Hammer's only goal has become beating the competition, indicating a shallow personality. Very much the bratty younger brother, Hammer enviously calls Tony "wonder boy" and calls Howard Stark "Really a father to us all." Like Loki, he is eaten up by spitefulness and envy—he must have all the hero has, become him in fact, or he cannot be satisfied. In Monaco, he takes a picture with Tony, while bragging that he has the same expensive car as he does, the same *Vanity Fair* interview, the same technology. Hammer's life revolves around Tony whereas Tony becomes Iron Man in spite of society's (particularly the US government's and military's) protests—he's saving people because he feels it's the right thing to do and to take responsibility for the destruction his weapons have caused. His reckless, fun-loving personality exists independent of Hammer and nearly oblivious to him. However, he has a bigger soul-crisis.

"Unfortunately the device that's keeping you alive is also killing you," JARVIS warns. Though Stark acts like his fun-loving self, his blood is becoming increasingly toxic underneath. "Should I Stay or Should I Go" plays in the background, indicating the crossroads he's approaching. While Tony considers the Stark Expo all-important, a chance for the world's best and brightest to collaborate, he's also obsessed with his legacy as he begins to die. "The actual process of individuation – the conscious coming-to-terms with one's own inner center (psychic nucleus) or self – generally begins with a wounding of the personality and the suffering that accompanies it" (Von Franz 169). This catapults Tony onto his adventure.

Though he's constructed a façade of competency, beneath he's turned into a bundle of conflicting impulses. As the problem echoes outward, he has four Iron Man suits in different colors, indicating his split. If he is Iron Man, as he says, being four iron men means being four selves, from CEO to philanthropist. He replaces a work of modern art, a single strong black line, with a fifth iron man image. His company is "in complete disarray," as Potts worries, with him diversifying more and more into new energy technologies. His company, like himself, is spread too thin. "Got any other bad ideas?" he asks the mirror hopelessly in

Monaco, fancy suit open to reveal all his layers, from the shining core on up. He wants to go on vacation in Venice, and cancel the birthday party he fears may be his last. "It's a great place to…be healthy," he says, a shadow literally falling over his face as he sits on the plane.

Tony begins to feel doubts over his heroism, his ability to handle all these diverging goals and pieces of his personality. In response, he splits off parts of his psyche, allowing Potts, his sense of responsibility, to inherit the company and Rhodey, his patriotic duty, to take his suit to the military. When Rhodey gives him a long searching look and then flies away in the older, silver version of the Iron Man suit, it's like the pure Iron Man part of Tony is abandoning him, leaving him crumpled and drunk on the floor of his club.

In the comics, writer David Michelinie and artist Bob Layton's landmark run in *Iron Man* #120–128 (March–November 1979), "Demon in a Bottle," sees Tony Stark face up to his alcoholism.

> In Michelinie's tense thriller, Stark's company is ever so slowly wrested from his grasp, while competing industrialist Justin Hammer frames Iron Man for the murder of a foreign ambassador on live television. Under constant pressure — he loses his company, and Iron Man's reputation is in ruins — Stark increasingly turns to alcohol. He eventually hits rock bottom, then finds the strength to turn away from the bottle. The subject is maturely handled, and Layton's art is clean and appealing. (Ryall and Tipton)

In the eighties, Tony Stark tumbles into a bottle again and Rhodes remains Iron Man for more than three and a half years, finally becoming War Machine when Tony reclaims his identity.

As described in flashback in "Apocalypse Then," Tony Stark becomes Iron Man during the Vietnam War. After building the suit and escaping his captors, Tony meets the American marine pilot Jim Rhodes. They fight side by side and save each other before discovering a secret rocket base and destroying it. Tony offers him a job after (though he doesn't reveal his secret identity yet) and Jim Rhodes becomes "his private pilot, his chief aviation engineer, and ultimately, his friend" (*Iron Man* #144).

While the previous film had Pepper Potts as Tony's loyal sidekick, this one shows Potts inheriting the company while she and Tony share a sidekick in the alluring, secretive Natasha. She first appears as paralegal Natalie Rushman, looking alluring in black and white beside Potts' more muddled grey. Tony is instantly attracted, and why not—her outfit echoes the clear certainty he's been losing. "I need someone now, I feel like it's her," he says, calling her an old soul with quiet reserve, the opposite of himself (of course, her job as an underwear model in Tokyo doesn't hurt).

Potts subsumes her entire life in Tony's, while her replacement is secretly using Tony for her own agenda. We have the repressed good girl and the morally dubious assassin and spy. The sweet one and the spicy one. In this way, the ladies polarize through the series, with Potts in elegant black and Natasha in cleavage-revealing red in Monaco. Potts is shown as a helpless female, more extremely than in the first movie as her hysterical screams block her from helping her hero. Natasha isn't thrown by anything, appearing more controlled and competent than Tony, who's quickly losing charge of his life.

Other foils for Tony appear in the shadow – all reflections of parts of himself he's suppressing. Wanting to regain the fun, daring side that's becoming an increasingly thin façade, Tony hops in a racecar and there he's confronted by all he's trying to forget. His enemy Ivan Vanko arrives as a second Iron Man, ripping Tony's fun-seeker persona to shreds as he demolishes the cars. He has lightning whips, tearing the world apart with that very electricity while Tony struggles to heal it. He seeks revenge, something Tony must rise above, acting to protect the world, not battle his enemies.

Vanko reflects the brutal side of Iron Man – the genius but only used for destruction. In *The Ultimates*, he appears in *Spider-Man* #150 as a terrorist seeking to kill Tony. The classic comics character, actually written only shortly before the Marvel film, seeks revenge for his father's death at the hands of an Iron Man imposter. Vanko reverse-engineers a suit from the imposter's, adds energy whips, and tries to murder Tony. Upon learning of Iron Man's innocence, Vanko tries again to kill him, claiming that even though he did not destroy the village, his technology did. He remains a voice of criticism and rage at Iron Man's existence. In the movie, Howard Stark arguably cheated his father, in both cases reminding Tony that big business doesn't succeed by playing nice.

After their battle in the film, his nemesis sits nearly naked in the dark, while Tony paces in black and a leather jacket, cool and articulate. "You come from a family of thieves and butchers," Vanko says, accusing Tony of trying to rewrite his own history. In a few words, this shadow self cuts through all of Tony's carefully crafted surfaces, especially the heroic image he's been selling the world of his father the peacemaker. He also sees that Tony is dying of palladium poisoning, confronting him with the truth he hides so carefully. In fact, this second Iron Man does more than see Tony's hidden flaws—he reveals them to all. Vanko insists he has attacked Tony because "if you can make God bleed…there will be blood in the water and the sharks will come." Tony's image is tarnished before the world, as the media babbles about his foolishly naïve assertion that he's the only Iron Man possible. His hidden self, all he's buried, is tearing him apart, shattering all the lies he tells himself to keep functioning.

Tony is the ultimate loner so Nick Fury appears, assembling a team of heroes and judging how well Tony might fit in. The mentor represents "the whole psyche, the larger and more comprehensive identity that supplies the strength that the personal ego lacks" (Henderson 101). It's Fury, himself strong and complete, who pins Tony down and makes him reassess. "You can solve the riddle of your heart," Fury tells him. While Tony's heart is literally failing, his deeper problem is a lack of direction and commitment.

Fury solves this by passing on his father's legacy and then locking him in his house without communications, forcing him to stop acting out through his friends and focus inward. Tony discovers that his father loved him and trusted him to carry on his legacy. Though deprived of the false too-perfect father Tony has been presenting to the world, he finds his real father and the gift he created for his son—a new chance at life. Anton Vanko "saw it as a way to get rich" while Tony's father truly does want to create world peace and a better future.

The house is a metaphor for the self, and the basement, the unconscious. "The cellar, one can say, is the basement of the dreamer's psyche" (Von Franz 176). To Jung, this level of the mind is "everything of which I know, but of which I am not at the moment thinking; everything of which I was once conscious but have now forgotten; everything perceived by my senses, but not noted by my conscious mind" (401). The answer to the puzzle exists within, waiting to be unlocked. Armed with this new knowledge, Tony does "a major remodel," tearing down walls with a drill and sledgehammer. As he remodels his house, he metaphorically remodels himself, fixing and reprioritizing to make a new identity. After extensive reworking, Tony fixes his heart and his Iron Man there in the basement of the self, confronting all the impulses he's been burying rather than facing. When he listens to the voices of his father, Pepper and all the others he's ignored, his creativity unfurls like a flower and he invents a new element, that will power his life and heart as well as the world. This is a descent into the inner world, leaving it renewed and filled with a replenished sense of understanding.

After Tony installs his improved chest device, Potts and Natasha arrive at the expo, now partners, dressed identically, walking in sync. The opposing sides of his personality have reconciled. Though Vanko controls Rhodes' suit, the women reboot Rhodes, and he returns firmly on Tony's side as his partner. With Rhodes besides him, and Natasha, Pepper and the chauffer Happy Hogan helping from the sidelines, Tony's many aspects are finally working together, strong and solid as his heart.

The second movie has no world-threatening bad guy, only scheming Vanko and Hammer – the threat is personal to Tony as both join to destroy his surface persona and reveal his patchwork of flaws to the world. Campbell describes facing this shadow as "destruction of the world that we have built and in which we live, and of ourselves within it; but then a wonderful reconstruction, of the bolder, cleaner, more spacious, and fully human life" (8). In fact, the plot ends with Tony proudly telling Nick Fury that he has his entire self under control and is no longer indulging in self-destructive tendencies. It seems that this is truly the deeper point of the film.

THE AVENGERS FACE THEIR DARK SIDES

Discovering the Inner Child: Iron Man 3

When we were developing *Iron Man* 1, a comic book came out called *Extremis*. It was written by Warren Ellis and drawn by Adi Granov and from the cover of the first issue, we realized it was the next level of *Iron Man* and it worked perfectly and the timing was perfect. We felt it was tonally something we could use to build the movie off of. We actually ended up hiring Adi Granov to come on board and help in the initial designs of the Iron Man armor for the film. (Keyes)

Extremis is a six-issue volume arc from *Iron Man* (vol. 4), 2005–2006. At Futurepharm Corporation offices in Austin, Texas, Dr. Aldrich Killian commits suicide at his computer. He leaves a confession admitting that he has released his Extremis serum for a greater purpose, so his coworker Maya Hansen contacts Tony Stark, whom she met years before. Maya tells Stark that Extremis, military nanotechnology serum, was another attempt to recreate the Captain America Serum by interfacing with the brain's "repair center" and directing the body to rebuild itself. Iron Man battles the first new Extremis super soldier, Mallen, who far surpasses Iron Man in strength and toughness. Tony is so injured from the fight that he needs Extremis to survive. Tony alters the serum to link himself to his armor physically and mentally. While thus upgraded, Tony can fold up the suit within the hollow spaces of his bones and even control it better, although the Extremis nanobots give him hallucinations and increased aggression. Battling Mallen once more, Iron Man compares them, pointing out that each of them has killed fifty people – Tony, trying to escape the terrorists in his own origin story, Mallen because he cares nothing for others.

Failing to convince him, Tony kills him quite violently. He then arrests Maya for her complicity. Maya then declares that Tony is no better than she is, to which Iron Man replies, "No. But I'm trying to be...And tomorrow I'll be able to look myself in the mirror." Writer/director Shane Black explains:

> In the Extremis comic book, there's a type of thing that takes over and basically upgrades DNA. Sometimes you die. But if you live through the experience then you come out this changed thing. But the way they do it is the guy that does it is not some man chosen to be the supersoldier – he's just a militia guy. There's an element of realism to it as well. So what we've tried to do is take this very science-fiction concept of super people, and ground it in the type of people who volunteer for this being not necessarily super villains, but just people who upgrade. I love the idea of a super villain that doesn't wear a cape, that doesn't wear a super suit. That goes around dressed as you are right now. As for the science of it, once again we've gone back to the comic books, and I think pretty much lifted the Maya Hensen idea, that she met [Tony] long ago and had the germ of an idea, which now has come to fruition full circle, but she's afraid because it's gotten out there. And we go from there. ... What we do keep from the comic is the idea that there's a slot in the brain that seems to have been dormant, but exists in human beings, almost as though it's waiting for human beings to find a way to fill it. It's been there forever." (Keyes)

During the 2012 *Believe* story arc, Maya Hansen is killed and new versions of Extremis are released onto the black market, leaving Tony to track them down and battle their users once more.

"We create our own demons. Who said that? What does that even mean? Doesn't matter. I said it 'cause he said it, so now if he was famous, then it's basically getting said by two well-known guys," Tony narrates at the film's beginning. In fact, Tony certainly creates his own dark reflections. The film starts with a flashback of his alienating AIM and its creator Aldrich Killian who becomes the film's supervillain. Guy Pearce, his actor, explains Killian's background, noting:

> Killian is an interesting character as he's somebody who came into this world with a number of physical disabilities. He's never been able to accept those limitations though and

has spent most of his life trying to overcome them in any way he can. His tenacity and blind determination in fighting for a better life are seen by some as irritating, as he often comes across as obnoxious. He just won't accept the cards he was dealt, and being as intelligent as he is, has real drive to change and become a different person.

So we find him at the start of the film in a flashback and we see the ambitious, almost annoying, guy that he is. He takes opportunities to try and latch onto people like Tony Stark. So you see this very ambitious character and you see him later on in the film having made a change, and Tony and the other people that have met him early on kind of go, "How did this happen? How did he do this?" But he's a dangerous character. He wants to become all-powerful. That's sort of a driving force with him and Tony Stark realizes eventually what this guy is capable of. (Keyes)

He of course is Tony's shadow, inventing technology that kills its users and fills the world with violence. While Tony battles him, Tony also spends the film suffering from panic attacks after his near death in *The Avengers*. This is a personal, internal struggle for the hero. He's also having trouble incorporating this moment of pure unselfishness and self-sacrifice, into his character, so once more he turns childish and hurtful, especially to Pepper.

Happy alerts Tony that his business and romantic rival Killian is wooing Pepper by inviting her into an image of his "giant brain." Happy, a voice of Tony's subconscious, tells him: "You know what? You should take more of an interest in what's going on here. This woman is the best thing that ever happened to you and you're just ignoring her."

By removing himself from the emotional world, wrapping himself in his suit on date night and hiding from Piper, Tony is allowing the intellect to make a play for her and risking his heart vanishing from the scene completely. He confesses to her:

Tony: I'm a piping hot mess. It's been going on for a while...
Pepper: I haven't said anything.
Tony: Nothing's been the same since New York. Oh really? I didn't notice that, at all. You experience things and then they're over and you still can't explain them. Gods, aliens, other dimensions...I'm just a man in a can. The only reason I haven't cracked up is probably because you've moved in. Which is great. I love you; I'm lucky. But honey... I can't sleep.

You go to bed, I come down here. I do what I know; I tinker.
The threat is imminent. And I have to protect the one thing
that I can't live without... That's you. And my suits; they're
uh...Machines. They're part of me.
Pepper: A distraction.
Tony: Maybe.

While Tony builds more and more "selves," the War Machine,
James Rhodes, has been rebranded as the Iron Patriot. He has a
single identity, a single suit. As with the second movie, he's a more
responsible reflection of heedless Tony, though Tony's breakdown
this time is mental, not physical. Feige explains:

> The Iron Patriot is also kind of a response to *Avengers*. It's a
> government rebrand of War Machine, frankly because the US
> government felt that they were slightly embarrassed by the
> events of *Avengers*. These crazy heroes known as "The
> Avengers" were the ones that saved the day, saved New York
> City, saved United States; not the government. The
> government felt they needed a hero of their own, they have a
> military officer that has one of these suits, and they paint it
> red, white, and blue. They pose it next to the president and
> Tony sort of rolls his eyes, you saw a little bit of that today.
> They want a hero of their own. And Tony's like, "What do you
> mean, I'm a hero?" And they say, "Well you've been spending
> a lot of time in your workshop. We want somebody we can
> rely on." (Weintraub)

Rhodes is the reliable Iron Man, Tony is the radical, emotional,
crumbling one. After the events of *The Avengers*, Tony Stark is truly
falling apart. His panic appears in a café as he eats with Rhodey and
hears that the world is still a mess with the Mandarin attacking. As
two children approach him for an autograph and one asks how he
got out of the wormhole, he shuts down. Rushing outside, he
climbs into the suit, treating it as both a blanket over his head (as
he shuts out the concerned world) and a medical diagnostic,
though it can only register him as physically fine.

Tony: Sorry. Have to check on the suit...make sure...Check
the heart, check the, check the, is it the brain?
JARVIS: No sign of cardiac anomaly or unusual brain activity
Tony: Okay, so I was poisoned?
JARVIS: My diagnosis is that you've experienced a severe
anxiety attack.

Tony: Me?
Rhodes: Come on man, this isn't a good look. Open up.
Tony: Sorry, I gotta split.

There's a heavy theme of childishness as Tony gets Pepper a giant stuffed rabbit as a Christmas gift and plays a prank on her, hanging out only as the suit so he can multitask downstairs. He creates another suit, framing it as a child: "Focus up ladies. Good evening and welcome to the birthing suite. I am pleased to announce the imminent arrival of your bouncing, badass baby brother." However, the pieces fly at him too fast, attacking him. Metaphorically, his suit has become his enemy as well as armor. "Come on. I ain't scared of you," he tells the mask, which in fact, slams itself into his face. His duty is becoming his enemy. Kevin Feige explains:

> The only real connective tissue we wanted from *Avengers* in this movie was *Avengers'* effect on Tony's psyche. This man who comes from this grounded universe ... now has been to outer space, nearly got killed by freaking aliens, has encountered a god that can smash him across the forest with a hammer, has encountered a guy that his father used to talk about from 1945. It's no mistake that we meet Tony at the beginning of this movie and he's just building suits, putting himself in the suit, and he's much more comfortable when he's in the suit. And a lot of this movie is about Tony learning to become Tony Stark again outside the armor, and he has a little help in that his house is completely destroyed. (Weintraub)

He even dares the Mandarin, a terrorist, to come attack his house. This in fact happens, destroying his entire facade of a life and plunging him under the ocean, utterly alone. "Instead of passing outward, beyond the confines of the visible world, the hero goes inward, to be born again" (Campbell 91). This plunge into the abyss is a metaphorical death, a loss of everything and chance to regroup.

After, Tony pulls himself from the water and returns to earth but only by exiling himself to Rose Hills, Tennessee. This is a place of no societal expectations, no duty, where Tony can listen to the quiet voices within: The suit, operating as always on what he needs rather than what his brain commands, carries him into the wilderness to find himself. He becomes a wanderer "and this in and of itself is a resurrection into a new life, and a death in the old" (Estés 445). Further, the suit takes him to the house of a child. Abandoned by a repairing JARVIS, with no adults around, Tony finds himself facing this child, Harley Keener (with a potato gun like he once had himself) who represents the immature abandoned part of Tony himself.

He and the child are mirror images: both invent things with electromagnets. Within minutes, the child is suggesting cool improvements for the suit like stealth mode while Tony criticizes the style of the potato gun. Tony perceptively notes that the kid is bullied at school and offers him a high-tech toy to solve his problem, fulfilling the fantasy of kids everywhere. He says he's offering the kid "salvation," but in fact the kid is doing the same for him.

Jungian scholar Joseph L. Henderson describes a man's encounter with a boy in the dream world, easily transferred to the world of superheroes: "The son in the dream is the man's own youthful ego, which had frequently felt threatened by the shadow in the form of self-doubt." Now, he has matured enough to accept this child as an ally not and enemy. This means "He is no longer driven to a competitive struggle for individual supremacy but is assimilated to the cultural task of forming a democratic sort of community" (119). In the film, young Harley soon zooms in on Tony's own problem:

> Harley: Oh my God! Is that Iron Man?
> Tony: Technically, I am.
> Harley: Technically, you're dead.
> Tony: A valid point.
> Harley: What happened to him?
> Tony: Life. I built him. I take care of him. I'll fix him.
> Harley: Like a mechanic.
> Tony: Yeah.

Thus Tony makes himself a new identity – not the Iron Man who can withstand anything, but humble Tony the mechanic, on a quest to fix Iron Man by fixing himself. Feige explains, "We had pillars of we want it to be: a Tony Stark-centric story, we want to blow up his life and see how he deals with a nemesis without his suits working, get him back metaphorically to the cave with a box of scraps, like the first movie" (Weintraub).

While Tony quickly arranges to fix the mechanics of his life, he's dismissive of the personal. When he hears that the kid, like himself, lost a dad at a young age, he says, "Which happens, dads leave. No need to be a pussy about it." He is certainly talking to the needy child inside himself. The kid however continues to try to make him share:

> Harley: When can we talk about New York?
> Tony: Maybe never, relax about it.
> Harley: What about the Avengers, can you talk about them?
> Tony: I don't know; later. Hey kid, give me more space.

The kid continues to push, not just for Tony to talk about his experience but to listen to the child voice inside himself, acknowledge its presence, and love it.

> Harley: Admit it: you need me. We're connected.
> Tony: What I need is for you to go home, be with your mom, keep your mouth shut, and protect the suit. And stay connected to the telephone because if I call you better pick up. Okay? Can you feel that? We're done here. Move out of the way or I'm going to run you over. Bye kid.

After the flippant violence of his mock threat, Tony backs away from his rejection, starting to reconcile with his inner child, at last a bit. "I'm sorry, kid. You did good."

> Harley: So now you're just going to leave you here, like my dad?
> Tony: Yeah. Wait, you're guilt-tripping me, aren't you?
> Harley: I'm cold
> Tony: I can tell. You know how I can tell? 'Cause we're connected.
> Harley: It was worth a shot.

The child is tougher than he appears, much like Tony's wounded inner self. Tony in turn tells him, "If you do someone a solid, don't be a yutz, alright, just play it cool. Otherwise you come off grandiose," advice he might have benefited from as a child.

Working together, Tony finds himself getting more childlike as he wears the Dora the Explorer watch and complains, "That belongs to my friend's sister!" He refers to the attacking thug as a "bully" and gets the child sidekick to take him out. When Tony has another panic attack on the thought of going into battle s just himself with no suit, the kid helps him through it, saying with youthful clarity, "You're a mechanic, right? … What don't you just build something?" At this moment, Tony realizes he doesn't need his armor when he has his creativity and imagination. With a steady, "Okay, thanks, kid," he charges into battle with an arsenal of handmade weapons.

Through his adventures, Tony's suit arrives in pieces, lacking power, and otherwise reflecting his dismembered state within. Shane Black sees him as desperate for his suits in this film, building more and bigger and better: "His comfort in his own skin has diminished at the start of this movie by the fact that he feels like, unless he can build the perfect man, he's going to be outdone and outshone by these people who are literally gods" (Weintraub). Nonetheless, he saves the day each time, even with only a glove and boot.

Nice again, Tony is caught between good girl and bad girl. "See we all begin wide-eyed… 'pure science.' Then the ego steps in, the obsession. And when you look up, you're a long way from shore," Maya Hansen tells Pepper.

Pepper responds of Maya's military contracts, "That's exactly what we used to do. So don't judge yourself." However, Maya betrays her moments later. Killian injects Pepper with Extremis to motivate Tony to correct its flaws. He also shoots Maya, his duped accomplice, when she balks. Tony tries to aid her, but must finally tell her, "I can't help you. You used to have a moral psychology. You used to have ideals. Wanted to help people, now look at you. I get to wake up every morning with someone who … still has a soul." He's turned his back on making weapons – Killian and Maya are like an echo of who he once was but will never be again. During the 2012 *Believe* story arc, Tony calls Maya, "the woman who managed to trick the military into funding a cure for pretty much everything thinking it was the ultimate killing machine … I'm the guy who spent his twenties making weapons." It's a delicate balancing act.

As Tony infiltrates the compound, he discovers the truth behind the brutal terror threat, the Mandarin. Tony understands him from the start. While JARVIS describes him as "His name is

an ancient Chinese war mantle. Meaning advisor to the King."
Tony notes: "South American insurgency tactics. Talks like a
Baptist preacher. There's lots of pageantry going on here... lots of
theatre." As he discovers at Killian's compound, there is no
Mandarin, only Trevor Slattery from England and some green
screens While Tony relies on his larger-than life presence, Killian's
weapon is anonymity, matching him with the Mandarin but only
operating behind the scenes. He likewise co-opts the iconic Iron
Patriot, putting one of his own men inside it to kidnap the
president. Shane Black explains:

> They're showmanship. They're accoutrements. They're
> paraphernalia of warfare that he sort of drapes himself with.
> He studies Sun Tzu. He studies insurgency tactics. He
> surrounds himself with dragons and symbols of warlords and
> Chinese iconography because he wants to represent this sort
> of prototypical terrorist who – we use as the example Colonel
> Kurtz from *Apocalypse Now* - this guy who may have been an
> American, may have been a British National, someone who is
> out there doing field work, supervising atrocities for the
> intelligence community who went nuts in the field and became
> this sort of devotee of war tactics, and now has surrounded
> himself with a group of people over which he presides, and
> the only thing that unifies them is this hatred of America. So
> he's the ultimate terrorist, but he's also savvy. He's been in
> the intelligence world. He knows how to use the media. And
> taking it to a real world level like that was a lot fun for
> us. (Weintraub)

"Iron Man battles alcoholism and Wolverine surmounts mental
illness. Each rises from his ashes like the proverbial phoenix. Each
becomes bigger and bigger after overcoming personal ordeals"
(Packer 39). However, after facing his demons – life as just a man,
the evil grandiosity of Killian, the simple trust of Pepper and the
kid, he refocuses his drive. He enters Air Force One and saves
civilians in the superhero's classic mission. As the mission
concludes, civilians safe and cheering for him, a single target left to
chase, he receives word that the basement of his old house has
been unearthed safely – together with all his suits. Then he and
Rhodey go after Killian, who's holding Piper and the president as
his "trophies." Having reassembled all the aspects of himself, Tony
orders up a "house party" – all his suits flying into battle. The

season of hope and rejuvenation has worked his magic as he tells JARVIS: "Target Extremis heat signatures. Disable with extreme prejudice. … What are you waiting for? It's Christmas. Take 'em to church."

However, his beloved Piper falls into a fiery pit and he cannot save her. As she vanishes, the enemy taunts him:

> Killian: I was so close to having her... perfect.
> Tony: Okay, okay, wait, wait, slow down, slow down. Okay, you're right. I don't deserve her. But here's where you're wrong: She was already perfect.

Tony pushes one of his many suits onto Killian and blows it. In fact, in the battle he blows many suits, acknowledging that they aren't the priority. Fiery Killian and protected, armored Tony are a match in more than power. One relies on tech that conceals the body while the other invites Piper into his brain and reconfigures his very body. He represents the physical, something like the inner child that Tony fears and separates himself from.

The Iron Man chest device is tech adapted to serve man – it does everything a human heart does and more, as it repels the shrapnel and powers the suit. However, as Maya Hansen describes Extremis in the comics:

> It's a bio-electronics package, fitted into a few billion graphic nanotubes and suspended in a carrier fluid. … It hacks the body's repair center—the part of the brain that keeps a complete blueprint of the human body. …. The normal human blueprint is being replaced with the Extremis blueprint, you see? The brain is being told the body is wrong. … Extremis uses the nutrients and body mass to grow new organs. Better ones. (*Iron Man* vol. 4 #3)

This doesn't serve man, it uses and redesigns him. Killian's test subjects become his drones, doing his bidding until it causes their deaths. Thus Tony Stark isn't just fighting biology-tech but evil tech. In the comics, he's implanted with this instead of Piper in the film.

However, Piper returns from the fiery pit thanks to her new powers plus an Iron Man glove. Pepper's brief time in a suit is a nod to her brief career as the superheroine Rescue in an "Invincible Iron Man" comic book series from 2009-2012. She pulverizes the enemy, only to break down with the words "That was really violent!" Unlike Tony, she does not enjoy all the firepower.

Tony promises Pepper he can save her, using once more his creativity and his brain. He blows up all his suits, in a moment that seems rather dramatic and pointless, except that he's vowing to Piper that he'll "cut down" on his "hobbies" and prioritize her, the real person in his life. "For Tony, the armor was a psychological crutch preventing him from dealing with his own inner demons," writer Denny O'Neil explains. "When he gets around to building his new armor, he sees it for what it should be, simply a tool" (Ridout 7).

After, he realizes from his adventures, that his power is internal and he doesn't need a suit or a shell. He gets the surgery to fix himself completely and become ordinary and human. Perversely, it seems on some level he's taken a lesson from Killian and prefers humanity to a superpowered body. In celebration, he sends lavish gifts to his inner child and gives Piper a heart-shaped necklace. As he concludes, finally stable and at peace:

> So if I were to wrap this up tight with a bow or whatever, I guess I'd say my armor was never a distraction or a hobby. It was a cocoon. And now, I'm a changed man. You can take away my house, all my tricks and toys. One thing you can't take away...I am Iron Man.

THE AVENGERS FACE THEIR DARK SIDES

Loving the Monster: The Incredible Hulk

The Hulk is arguably the most powerful of the Avengers. Grant Morrison notes in his book, "The low production costs (pen and ink can conjure scenes that would cost millions of dollars of computer time to re-create onscreen) and rapid publication frequency mean that in comic books, almost anything goes. No idea is too bizarre, no twist too fanciful, no storytelling technique too experimental" (xvi). Though the Hulk is difficult to produce, he's had a television show and several films, one just before the MCU franchise began.

Hulk (2003) is directed by Ang Lee, with Eric Bana as Dr. Bruce Banner, with Jennifer Connelly, Sam Elliott, Josh Lucas, and Nick Nolte. In a story somewhat removed from the dynamic of the comics, Bruce's father is the one to have mutated him as well as himself, and finally admits that he murdered his wife in front of the child Bruce. He and Bruce end the film with a superfight between their Hulked-out selves that reflects their animosity, now externalized.

For the MCU franchise, a reboot as *The Incredible Hulk* (2008) was the second film released. Marvel Studios reacquired the rights, and Zak Penn wrote the script, though Edward Norton rewrote Penn's script substantially after he signed on to star. While his transformation into the Hulk is shot as a quick preview, emphasizing that this film *might* be a sequel to the previous one, it's really not. Bruce's father is not a character, and Bruce has injected himself through hubris – playing God without suspecting the possible repercussions. Liv Tyler, Tim Roth, Tim Blake Nelson, Ty Burrell, and William Hurt also star. The film hit No. 1 at its box office release and Norton was intended to portray Banner again in the films that followed, but after talks broke down, he was replaced by Mark Ruffalo, who has signed on to reprise the role in future Marvel films. Despite the recasting afterwards, *The Incredible Hulk* was created as an MCU film, with Tony Stark in a cameo at the end to bring up the Avengers Initiative. Thus this chapter will analyze the film as the origin story of Bruce Banner from *The Avengers*.

Stan Lee envisioned the Hulk as the central figure in his original concept. As he tells it, "There would only be one superhero. Oh, and by the way – I wanted that hero to be a monster" (Lee and Mair 120). First came the misunderstood Frankenstein who doesn't want to hurt the villagers, but they won't stop attacking. Only next came Hulk's secret identity – Bruce Banner. As Lee adds, Jack Kirby on request drew "a monster who was so perfect, so empathetic, that the readers took to him immediately and today he's still one of our most popular heroes" (Lee and Mair 122). The monster is an important psychological figure, as the catalyst for personal growth. "To encounter the monster by engaging it in combat or by taming it implies action originating from the [hero] but engulfment implies action by being acted upon...But this transformation, insofar as it passes through symbolic death, also means a new beginning" (Beaudet 221). Having the monster burst from Banner challenges him to recognize this emerging part of himself and transform.

In the original comics, the first glimpse of the Hulk is shocking: He towers head and shoulders over the humans with a corpse-gray face like Frankenstein's. He appears at night, returning to Banner in the morning. Stan Lee explains, "Where Dr. Banner had been gentle, the Hulk was a brute! Where had been civilized, the Hulk was a savage! Where Banner was a man, the Hulk was a monster!" (#2).

"At first, the Hulk is merely confused and brutish, like a force of nature unleashed on an unsuspecting world. Soon, however, the Hulk grows bitter and angry" (Brewer 26). In comic #2, he captures an alien spaceship and notes, "With this flying dreadnaught under me, I can wipe out all mankind!" When Betty Ross asks the Hulk why he hates them, the Hulk responds, "Why shouldn't I hate you? Why shouldn't I hate all mankind? Look what men have done to me!" "The conscious personality here has come in touch with a charge of unconscious energy which it is unable to handle and must now suffer...while learning how to come to terms with this power of the dark and emerge, at last, to a new way of life," Joseph Campbell explains (146). Filled with the monster, Hulk struggles to become Banner once more. He was soon switched to green, but the series only lasted six issues. The Hulk, rejected by the comics audience as he was by society, got an ongoing strip in another comic; the Hulk took half the pages each month and another superhero, the other half. "In a weird parallel of the Hulk's relationship with Bruce Banner, eventually the Hulk's strip squeezed out the other comic feature and took over the book entirely" (Brewer 29). Over the next four decades, his comics were published without interruption.

The film introduces Banner living in Brazil. Ironically, he makes bright, chemically green potions...in the form of soda. One bottle becomes contaminated with his gamma irradiated blood, making the soda as deadly as it looks (as Stan Lee in his traditional cameo is the one to drink it).

While Banner is certainly fleeing his old life – hiding in obscurity with a menial job, separated by his skin color and the language barrier – he's also wearing it on his sleeve by working in the glowing green soda plant. Likewise, as he seeks help anonymously on the web, his code name is Mr. Green (his counterpart, Mr. Blue suggests calming reassurance).

Banner's tools – computer, centrifuge, microscope, and heart monitor – all emphasize man's attempt to control his body. "Banner is a well-meaning man, a believer in reason and logic, and he trusts his own ability to control the Hulk and eventually to cure himself. Nonetheless, every attempt to tame the Hulk fails" (Brewer 27). Edward Norton adds:

> The story isn't really ultimately about the Hulk, it's about Bruce Banner. It's anchored in that character, because the thing that people loved, even in the television show I think, is the story of a maligned and oppressed and persecuted and hunted man who is moral, who is trying to contain this thing, to protect other people from it, who in a lot of senses is an exile, who has this righteous kind of bite-back when you push him too hard... And I think that when you're young that taps a lot of feelings, that feeling of being alienated or exiled or out in the cold. There's a great fantasy that you have when you don't feel empowered, that you have this lurking monster within you that's going to come out to defend you if people

hassle you... It's a fantasy a lot of teenagers can relate to! Not just teenagers...

"The monster mediates the archetypal realm, bringing the underside of life to expression" (Beaudet 219). He is the gateway to deeper knowledge, a smasher of barriers and the rules of civilized life. Thus he offers the shrimpy human within a chance for growth.

Banner has a shadow in the first act – not only the Colonel chasing him but also the more aggressive thug and his cronies who work beside Banner at the plant. One flirts aggressively with a woman, forcing Banner to step in and protect her. The thug also represents rage, though he makes no attempt to hide it. As he menaces Banner, the language parallels, each warning the other that if they get angry thing will be "bad." Of course Banner means something far more serious. But as his shadow jumps him at the worst time and strips him of the laptop and watch of his rationality, the thug tears the raging beast from helpless Banner, giving him the excuse to act on his secret desires and unleash his rage.

"The shadow cast by the conscious mind of the individual contains the hidden, repressed and unfavorable (or nefarious) aspects of the personality." However, "Just as the ego contains unfavorable and destructive attitudes, so the shadow has good qualities – normal instincts and creative impulses" (Henderson 110). The shadow is a catalyst for the hero to grow and act, and thus starts Bruce on his journey.

Bruce Banner is the skinny, geeky genius who's always been picked on – the Hulk is his power brought to life. On many levels he likes it even as it scares him. "Brains don't win fights! Banner had brains and people walk all over Banner! Strong the only one that counts – and Hulk the strongest one there is," the Hulk decides (*The Ultimates: Homeland Security*). Director Louis Lettier explains that this story focuses on Bruce's humanity:

Very early on [screenwriter] Zak [Penn] and I – before anybody was involved with the project – conceived the story as, "Let's find the best story about a guy who has a disease, but he doesn't have to be the Hulk. And then we'll put the Hulk in." At first, I want to find the emotional connection of the character and how people can relate with him. So we decided to tell Bruce Banner's story before telling the Hulk's.

The Hulk first appears in the soda plant. All is shadow – a foot, a growl, and finally his bestial face. As it plunges from the darkness, it seems a product of nightmare, but also one of the unconscious world. After the fight, his roar stretches across a wooded area, suggesting his connection to nature and the wilderness.

In fact, Banner awakens in the wilderness, mostly naked, in a place of Edenic paradise. The Hulk has torn him from his urban hiding place and restored him to the renewal of nature. Banner cannot continue to exist in a menial job, ignoring his problem, but must go out on the epic quest.

The villains are willing to sacrifice the Hulk, much like the reporter after him on the show. All claim they are the heroes while the Hulk is the villain, but the "heroes" display cruelty and treachery as the Hulk saves lives, throwing everything into doubt. The Hulk of course is the military's embarrassing, uncontrollable child and thus their own shadow, even as they seek to cage and destroy him. "Such self-righteous denial of one's own shadow side is what makes the pursuer a terribly misguided individual who cannot perceive the harm he is doing to others, and most of all, himself, by engaging in the hunt so blindly" (Iaccino 170).

General Ross is his adversary as patriarchy, the one who engineered him to be what he is. He then turns the aggressive Blonsky, a career soldier, into a supersoldier. As the general tells Blonsky that Banner, a peaceful scientist not told of military applications for his research "isn't one of us," he emphasizes their roles as warmongers.

His violent urge for dominance and world destroying with the Hulk grow so overwhelming that he summons all the might of the military, even when his daughter rushes into the combat zone. Only the Hulk manages to protect her by covering her. The Hulk's scream of rage at the general emphasizes that he realizes what treachery the man has committed.

While Banner is Hulked, his stand in and foil, Betty's psychologist boyfriend, is the one to confront the general on his behalf.

> Ross: I give you my word that her safety is my main concern at this point.

> Samson: You know it's a point of professional pride with me
> that I can always tell when somebody is lying. ... I used to
> wonder why she never talked about you...now I know.

The Hulk carries the unconscious Betty from the assault and takes
her to a cave in Smoky Mountain National Forest, retreating to
nature once more. "The Hulk is truly a repulsive brute, and his
story is ugly" (Brewer 24). In this scene, he certainly appears a
gawky, inhuman creature. Still, as he bangs his head on the cave
ceiling and, startled, hurls a bolder at the sky, he's not a force of
evil. He's nature incarnate, instinct and drive rather than the
calculating warmongers of the military. He's also frightened and
traumatized without any filters. To Jungian scholars, though, the
raging, rejected shadow has valuable qualities:

> Envy, lust, sensuality, deceit, and all known vices are the
> negative, "dark" aspect of the unconscious, which can
> manifest itself in two ways. In the positive sense, it appears
> as a "spirit of nature," creatively animating Man, things, and
> the world....In the negative sense, the unconscious (that same
> spirit) manifests itself as a spirit of evil, as a drive to destroy.
> (Jaffé 316).

In the forest, the Hulk is more spirit of nature than evil – he
protects Betty from the forces of civilization. Though he seems
little more than a wounded animal, Betty holds his hand and
soothes him. She wakes to find he's human once more. The story
from the first is a Beauty and the Beast tale, as Banner obsesses
over his lost girlfriend and keeps her picture nearby, even in exile.
Now Beauty and the Beast hide in hotels and stolen cars, removed
from society as she protects her charge.

> Betty Ross: What is it like? When it happens, what do you
> experience?
> Bruce Banner: Remember those experiments we volunteered
> for at Harvard? Those induced hallucination? It's a lot like
> that, just a thousand times amplified. It's like someone poured
> a liter of acid into my brain.
> Betty Ross: Do you remember anything?
> Bruce Banner: Just fragments. Images. There's too much
> noise. I can never derive anything out of it.
> Betty Ross: But then it's still YOU inside of it.
> Bruce Banner: No. No, it's not.

Betty Ross: I don't know. In the cave, I really felt like it knew me. Maybe your mind is in there, it's just overcharged and can't process what's happening.
Bruce Banner: I don't want to control it. I want to get rid of it.

In the earliest comics Banner invents a machine to change him back and forth, but the Hulk personality grows ever-stronger. He gradually comes to realize that the Hulk isn't an outside force, but all the dark side he's repressed. Reason, compromise, and cooperation vanish, replaced by fury.

> Most terrible of all for Bruce Banner is the dawning realization that the Hulk isn't a separate entity at all. The bestial Hulk represents the hidden dark side of Banner's own subconscious mind, the angry and aggressive persona Banner has always feared and repressed. Suddenly the habits and safeguards of a lifetime are inadequate. Morality, cooperation, acceptance, reason, compromise—all the bricks that build a civilized society—are shattered and scattered by the fury of the Hulk. (Brewer 28)

The horror of the story comes from Banner's realization that this creature has always existed within him. As Dr. Sterns (Mr. Blue) says on meeting Banner, "what would it look like...a person with that much power...lurking in him. Nothing could have surprised me more than this unassuming man shaking my hand!" Everyone, it seems, has such a force concealed within. Norton adds:

> Hulk isn't so much about desires or baser desires, but I do think it's about primal emotion. There's that part of your brain, the Amygdala, which is like the fear center, that's very, very primal, that's like been in use since long before we were human in a way. And I think that idea of like latent primal rage in everybody, that idea of hidden power and of unleashing... that is great.

Most people bury the shadow, but Banner's has gained too much power and it bursts out when Banner is threatened, much like a normal person's shadow but much, much darker. "The major question posed in *The Incredible Hulk* was that would happen if a scientist was able to tap into the hidden strengths shared by all mortals" (Iaccino 168). The comics emphasize how Banner's personal issues, exacerbated by the drugs, have made him this way:

> Only many years later in the story of the Hulk do we learn the cause of Bruce Banner's inner anger. A violent and alcoholic father physically and emotionally victimized young Bruce. Too small and weak to strike back at his father. Banner swallowed his rage and resolved never to follow in the old man's footsteps. Unlike his abusive father, Bruce Banner devoted himself to self-control and personal discipline. He eschewed violence and committed himself to the path of dispassionate reason.
>
> Banner's plan worked, or so it seemed. Unfortunately, anger and hate don't disappear just because we ignore them. Eventually Banner's long-denied feelings emerge with a vengeance—a gamma-powered vengeance. Tragically, the victim becomes the victimizer. The inner monster Bruce Banner kept tightly chained for so many years finally escapes and runs amok. (Brewer 28-29)

Sterns reflects who Banner once was – a mild mannered indoor scientist and genius in biology, eager to break the laws of science even at potentially fatal risk to himself. He's eager to cure the Hulk, ignoring the chance he'll be killed in the process. Norton notes, "There's a thing in *Hulk* of the Proteus myth: it's tapping the story of stealing fire from the gods and being burned by it… being empowered but then being exiled because of having taken that forbidden energy." This Sterns shares. However, he soon reveals that, seeking a Nobel Prize, he's amassed and created enormous quantities of Hulk-infected blood. He ends the film with a little splashed on him, and a bestial, jutting brow erupting. Those who try to rise above nature often sink below it.

The real threat is Blonsky, already a supersoldier, who adds Hulk powers to the deadly cocktail within. He becomes a bigger, scarier Hulk just as Bruce Banner hopes that Sterns has managed to cure him. All film, Bruce has been avoiding transformation and struggling to eliminate the beast forever. He considers him a curse with nothing beneficial to offer mankind, especially in war. Norton adds:

> When you think about Banner's driving motivation, part of what was interesting to me was a sense of guilt, a sense of

having monkeyed with nature. He's applied a certain arrogance to his work and assumed that he can master forces that maybe aren't meant to be tinkered with casually and he's driven by guilt in a way, or driven by a sense of wanting to put the genie back in the bottle. I think that's part of the theme of it, even with Abomination, that there's a certain blowback to messing around with nature. I thought that was fun about it, too.

Jung explains that the shadow personifies everything a person refuses to acknowledge about himself. Though these qualities go largely unseen in the hero, he must face them in the monster and acknowledge their place in his life. Jung notes:

The individual who wishes to have an answer to the problem of evil, as it is posed today, has need, first and foremost of *self-knowledge*, that is, the utmost possible knowledge of his own wholeness. He must know relentlessly how much good he can do, and what crimes he is capable of, and must beware of regarding the one as real and the other as illusion. Both are elements within his nature, and both are bound to come to light in him, should he wish – as he ought – to live without self-deception or self-delusion. (330).

Only by knowing his capacity for destruction can Banner go forward as a scientist and human being. The Hulk is the one to teach him this lesson.

However, when the Abomination, spoiling for a fight as Blonky's violent personality magnified, strikes Harlem, Banner bravely volunteers to stop him. For the first time, he takes responsibility for what he's created and calls his Hulk self "I," admitting that the beast is himself, and finally accepting it into his conscious life. The beast is not something to repress or kill but a tool he can command and use for a virtuous goal. If the Hulk is his guilt, the Abomination is his worst nightmare – others finding the technology and using it to bring supersoldiers into the world.

In the battle that follows, he is the "good Hulk," appearing far more human-shaped than the freakishly warped Abomination. He fights to preserve life, especially Betty and her father in the helicopter, while Blonsky only wants "a real fight" against the Hulk, and tries to destroy the helicopter, to say nothing of other innocents in Harlem. The Abomination is obviously the Hulk's shadow – Banner goes to Sterns for a cure, and Blonsky to become a weapon. Once transformed, Blonsky acts on many of Banner's and even the Hulk's hidden impulses and seeks to destroy Banner's enemy, the General, as well as the urban world of New York.

By creating this creature as the villain, the film gives the Hulk a chance to be the hero, the "good one" and use his violence for good. Norton explains:

> The whole fun of Hulk is the ass-kicking of it, that's the whole point – the thrill of it is knowing that if you push this guy, this quiet moral person, his bite-back is going to be legendary! And that is the entire fun of it – in fact it's an important part of it. The whole point of the comics, in a way, is that what Banner's terrified of is what Hulk does to the world and to people around him. We wanted the action to be a lot bigger in scale, to be the things that are really thrilling about the comic, which is Hulk going up against a lot of hardware, a lot of people and a really formidable enemy.

The Hulk uses his powers to end destruction, blowing out the flame about to engulf the chopper. Preserving those around him, he saves Betty and her father, and fights with his wits, not blind rage. He finally subdues the Abomination, uttering his first words of the film, "Hulk, Smash!" as he shatters the ground around him and traps his foe. The Hulk strangles him with his own chain weapon, but at Betty's urging, stops before committing murder. If the Abomination represents his capacity for destruction, Betty is his guardian angel. He listens to her, then touches her face and says her name before running to freedom once more.

Banner ends the film meditating in British Columbia, back in the wilderness that represents his home. He's meditating as he was at the film's beginning, but all has crucially changed. Now he accepts the Hulk as a tool to be controlled and soothed but not destroyed altogether. His eyes flash green and he smiles, welcoming the creature at last.

The Avengers has him terrified of "the other guy," whom he treats as the distant, unapproachable, unknowable shadow. He appears proven right when, frightened, he changes, and then attacks Natasha in the closed-in hold of the ship. Whedon explains in the DVD Commentary that Hulk attacks Black Widow to emphasize his lack of control and heroism as the monster.

However, this becomes a story of the way people choose to handle their rage.

> "We wanted to go with a Bruce Banner who isn't self-obsessed," Whedon says. "When Bruce Banner spends all his time trying to cure himself, he becomes that whiny guy that's getting in the way of your Hulk movie." So instead Ruffalo plays him like a recovering addict who's trying to get on with his life; meanwhile, his teammates need the Hulk's strength and Banner's scientific expertise, but they're terrified of his anger. "Is he a superhero or a monster?" Whedon says. "He's both." (Grossman)

In the final battle, Banner smiles as he strides into war. Ordered to "smash," he takes a life-affirming glee in his abilities, no longer holding back but embracing his rage and using it as a weapon to defend the innocents of Earth. As the monster, he aims himself at an empty building to protect innocents and as the monster he saves Tony Stark. The Hulk is learning to be mankind's savior, a valued member of the Avengers at last.

Embarking on the Hero's Journey: Captain America

In March 1941, Timely Comics (later to become Marvel Comics) published Captain America no. 1 by Joe Simon and Jack Kirby. With its bold attacks on the Nazis—and Hitler in particular—Captain America was a distillation of all the propaganda messages current at the time. Moreover, the comic itself was a form of propaganda, calling for intervention at a time when America was not yet at war, the first issue appearing months before the Japanese attack on Pearl Harbor. (131)

At the time, substitute enemies were common in comics, but Cap literally took on Hitler, right on his front cover. As a side note, Stan Lee's first published work was "Captain America Foils the Traitor's Revenge" in 1941's *Captain America* #3, long before he revived the character as a member of the Avengers in 1964.

The comics character Steve Rogers was born in Manhattan's Lower East side on July 4, 1917 on Independence Day. He's all-American, and in the film, he appears an ordinary guy. He's only special for his "heart," as he's tougher in the face of bullying and incredibly determined to enlist. He's courageous but nonviolent – as he tells Professor Erskine, "I don't want to kill anyone. I don't like bullies. I don't care where they're from."

Erskine replies, "Well, there are already so many big men fighting this war. Maybe what we need now is a little guy," and signs him up for special projects in SSR. As Colonel Phillips later explains, "The Strategic Scientific Reserve is an allied effort. Made up with the best minds of the free world. Our goal.

is to create the best army in history." He believes they will win the war with the "best men," and thus is the metaphoric best place for Rogers, the recruit who's best on the inside. Erskine takes him because, as he insists, "I am looking for qualities beyond the physical." He tells Steve just before the procedure, "Whatever happens tomorrow, you must promise me one thing. That you must stay who you are. Not a perfect soldier. But a good man."

Even after his transformation, Steve's idealism and heart are his predominating characteristics. Chris Evans notes, "Well, he is a really human superhero. He doesn't shoot lightning. He doesn't fly. It's very meat and potatoes type powers" (Keyes). At times he even resists the title, noting: "I never wanted to be Captain America. I was just supposed to be a soldier ... I just wanted to serve" in "Must There Be a Captain America?" (*Captain America* #616, May 2011). Evans adds:

> Sure, well, he feels comfortable within the structure that he's given. He likes to serve. He likes to take orders. He's like a herding dog. He needs a task. And I think the issue in the first two, *Captain America* and *The Avengers* – well, *Captain America* was about giving him the opportunity. Then he got the opportunity, and then he was thrust into a different world. (Keyes)

In the alternative future of *The Chosen*, Cap tells of his desire to serve with the troops rather than merely be a USO attraction for them: "I convinced the War Department that the only way I intended to cooperate was by taking the risks the others did. Those men didn't have super-powers. They were the true heroes" (*Captain America: The Chosen*, 2008). He also praises and finally passes on his spirit to America's unsung heroes: firefighters, doctors, teachers, and others: "Decent, caring people willing to sacrifice. Some of them are already heroes, although they don't think of themselves that way. They insist they're just doing their job."

Typically, the young hero in myth and other epic tales is likewise set apart by his inner qualities. He crosses into a magical world where his mentor trains him and gives him a magical weapon, leading to a transformation into a gifted crusader for goodness.

As Joseph Campbell describes his monomyth, also called the hero's journey or chosen one plot, in *The Hero with a Thousand Faces*

(1949): "A hero ventures forth from the world of common day into a region of supernatural wonder: fabulous forces are there encountered and a decisive victory is won: the hero comes back from this mysterious adventure with the power to bestow boons on his fellow man" (23).

Step one, the Call to Adventure, follows the hero into the magical realm. Campbell scholar Christopher Vogler explains, "The hero is presented with a problem, challenge, or adventure to undertake. Once presented with a Call to Adventure, she can no longer remain indefinitely in the comfort of the Ordinary World" (15). Traditionally, the call signals "the awakening of the self," an eagerness to become something more (Campbell 51). Cap undergoes the classic hero's journey in every particular – miserable and orphaned in the "real world" he enters the magical space of a carnival and there finds a unique opportunity. It's even called Project Rebirth. As Campbell notes:

> This fateful region of both treasure and danger may be variously represented: as a distant land, a forest, a kingdom underground, beneath the waves, or above the sky, a secret island, lofty mountaintop, or profound dream state; but it is always a place of strangely fluid and polymorphous beings, unimaginable torments, superhuman deeds, and impossible delight. The hero can go forth of his own volition to accomplish the adventure...or he may be carried or sent abroad by some benign or malignant agent....The adventure may begin as a mere blunder...or still again, one may be only casually strolling when some passing phenomenon catches the wandering eye and lures one away from the frequented paths of man. (58)

Elderly bearded Erskine appears the classic mentor from every hero story – he tests the young hero and recognizes his heart, then gives him the magical weapon needed to fight evil and face the story's supervillain – Excalibur or a lightsaber. In this case, the magical gift as the superserum, soon rendered unique. This "magic potion" allows Steve to become the warrior he's always dreamed, with enough heft and musculature to match his inner courage.

The comic shows Professor Reinstein (clearly modeled on Einstein) directly injecting the reader with the serum as a signal the young reader should come join in the fight "suggesting that by reading the comic and being filled with the patriotic message it contains, the reader can be transformed, like Captain America and the nation itself, suddenly prepared for the coming conflict" (Murray, "Propaganda" 136). Packer describes "Cap's significance in aiding the war effort and in encouraging otherwise thin or timid young men to enlist in the military" (121). A Nazi spy kills Professor Reinstein, leaving Cap unique in the world. He kills the spy, dons a stars and stripes costume and the rest is history.

Friends and allies are crucial to the hero, representing the little voices in one's head – self-confidence, logic, emotion. Onscreen, Bucky appears an older brother – he goes to war first and is much larger than Steve before his transformation. (In the comics, Bucky was Cap's "young ally" and sidekick, in a black eyemask like Robin's.) Film Bucky is a good friend and also insightful:

> Steve: Bucky come on, there are men laying down their lives. I got no right to do any less than them. That's what you don't understand. This isn't about me.
> Bucky: Right. 'Cause you got nothing to prove.

When Steve tells the brave and competent Peggy Carter that he was asked to stay in a lab, and that serving his country by selling war bonds is better than nothing, Peggy asks: "And these are your only two options? A lab rat or a dancing monkey? You were meant for more than this, you know." By cheerleading him, she encourages him to become a real soldier. Since she's the one to reveal that Bucky's division has been lost, she's that part of him eager to go to war, the little voice inside urging him to become more than a stage performer in his costume. In fact, she and Howard Stark fly him behind the lines as he charges off on a secret mission to rescue his friend. Dressed down afterwards by Colonel Phillips, she insists she doesn't regret her actions, adding, "I had faith."

Adding to the friends that help complete his personality, Cap learns the value of teamwork as he recruits the Howling Commandos and leads them into battle after battle. Stan Lee describes them as "the most ethnically mixed platoon I could dream up. It consisted of Jewish Izzy Cohen, Italian Dino Manelli, Irish Dum-Dum Dugan, Gabriel Jones, a Black man – well, you get the idea. There was even a gay platoon member named Percival Pinkerton" (Lee and Mair 162). While in life and in the film, this variety shines a light on Golden Age racism and encourages a better way of thinking, it also symbolizes many perspectives used to fuel an effective team. Cap's plan to stop the supervillain involves his walking into a trap and being taken prisoner…and relying on his friends to come save him – exactly what happens.

Earlier in the film, Erskine describes the supervillain as "the head of Hydra…a brilliant scientist by the name of Johann Schmidt.," and adds:

> Erskine: Now Schmidt is a member of the inner circle. And he's ambitious. Even Hitler shares his passion for occult power and Teutonic myth. Hitler uses his fantasies to inspire his followers. But for Schmidt it is not fantasy. For him, it is real. He has become convinced that there is a great power. Hidden in the earth. Left here by the gods. Waiting to be seized by superior men. So when he has found my formula and what it can do. He cannot resist. Schmidt wants to become that superior man.
> Steve: Did it make him stronger?
> Erskine: Ja. But, it has other effects. The serum wasn't ready. But more important. The man. The serum amplifies everything that is inside, so… Good becomes great. Bad becomes worse. This is why you were chosen. Because a strong man. Who has known power all his life. They lose respect for that power. But a weak man. Who values of strength. And loves compassion…

As Cap faces his adversary, Schmidt removes his face to reveal he's been transformed into a horrific red skull from the neck up. This is a trace of gothic horror straight from Dracula or Frankenstein – the embodiment of death, grotesque and monstrous. "The Red Skull is also reminiscent of the figure of death seen stalking the battlefields in much propaganda, often as a critique of enemy war-mongering or unscrupulous weapons manufacturers who benefit from war" (Murray, "Propaganda" 139). Early Cap comics were filled with gothic horror, representing the monstrousness of the enemy, as Cap fought brutish Nazis in a form of war propaganda. "The mythic structure of rhetoric, imagery, and symbolism employed by superhero comics were also central to propaganda" (Murray, Champions of the Oppressed 84). The Red Skull lived in medieval torture chambers, while Hitler lived in Gothic castles.

"The Riddle of the Red Skull," fourth comic in the collection that introduced Captain America, saw him facing a monstrous adversary in a grotesque red skull mask. He clutches his prey and tells them to "look at death" as they mysteriously die of no clear cause. Cap discovers he's an American traitor named Maxon, armed with a needle of poison. In the struggle, he allows Maxon to fall on the needle and die. Soon enough, however, a new Red Skull arrives as a Nazi supervillain.

The supervillain, just like friends and mentor, represents a part of the hero. Facing this abomination is like facing the savagery and lust for war and death within himself just as Steve takes his first step onto the battlefield. Steve is just becoming a soldier and can no longer be a "nice guy," but must shoot and kill the enemy. For this, he needs to invoke the hidden darkness within, the shadow, personified as Red Skull. Schmidt tells Steve, "You are deluded, Captain. You pretend to be a simple soldier. But in reality you are just afraid to admit that we have left humanity behind. Men like you. They embrace it proudly. No fear." They have their confrontation on a split bridge, emphasizing the widening gulf between them – hero and villain.

Nonetheless, the pair share a deeply symbolic connection. In the later comics, the newest incarnation of Red Skull thinks, "The two of us, locked in eternal combat down through the years...keeping each other miserable. What would we even *be* without the other?" (*Winter Soldier*).

Stan Lee's *Tales of Suspense Featuring Iron Man and Captain America* #80 follows Cap and Red Skull's battle for the Cosmic Cube "which can convert thought waves into material action" as the ultimate power source, clearly inspiring some of the film's plot. Onscreen, the Red Skull's tool is the Tesseract Cube, abandoned on earth by the gods of Asgard. Claiming it not only ties the franchise together but reveals his brutality and arrogance, all that is counter to compassionate Steve Rogers.

> Schmidt: The tesseract was the jewel of Odin's treasure room. It's not something one buries. But I think it is close, yes.
> Priest: I cannot help you.
> Schmidt: No. But maybe you can help your, uh village? You must have some friends out there. Some little grandchildren, perhaps. You have no need for them to die. [sees the wall image] Yggdrasil. The Tree of the world. Guardian of wisdom. And fate for some. And the Fuhrer digs for trinkets in the

desert. [takes the box and opens it] You have never seen this.
Have you?
Priest: It's not for the eyes of ordinary men.
Schmidt: Exactly. Give the order to open fire.
Priest: Fool. You cannot control the power you hold. You will
burn.
Schmidt: I already have.

By contrast, Steve's powers are entirely human, offered to him by
science, not stolen from the gods of myth.

Unlike the selfless hero, Schmidt is all ego, insisting, "Great
power has always baffled primitive men" and turning on his allies
to murder the Nazis who doubt him. When he takes Cap prisoner,
he reveals more insight, saying, "Arrogance may not be a uniquely
American trait. But I must say you do it better than anyone. But,
there are limits, to what even you can do, Captain. Or did Erskine
tell you otherwise?" Light glinting onto his skull from the tesseract
and darkening him, Schmidt tells Steve: "You could have the
power of the gods. Yet you wear a flag on your chest and think you
fight a battle of nations. I have seen the future, Captain. There are
no flags."

"Not my future," Cap retorts. He destroys the technology and
with it, Red Skull's seductive words. Having faced the savagery
within the enemy and also himself, he steps away and passes the
test: He is content to be just "a kid from Brooklyn" not a tyrant.
To bring down the villain, he hurls the too-dangerous cube into the
water, and finally crashes the entire ship in the ocean to save his
country, all while bidding Peggy a touching goodbye.

Death and rebirth is the climax of the hero's journey. In the
underworld, the "old self must perish in order for a new, stronger
personality to spring forth" (Frankel, *From Girl to Goddess* 126). This
is a dark initiation, as the hero perishes only to gain a more mature
self when he returns to a world of new possibilities. Steve's death is
quite literal, followed by a new world indeed – that of the future.

His time in the ice is straight from the comics, of course.
"With the decline in popularity of costumed superheroes in the late
1940s, Captain America's title folded and, apart from a brief revival
in 1954, the character wasn't seen in action again until Stan Lee
introduced him into *The Avengers* in 1964" (Reynolds 44). The ice
plot was included to explain his lack of aging in twenty years, while
his appearance in 1954 was quietly forgotten. Thus he became an

THE AVENGERS FACE THEIR DARK SIDES

Avenger, with a new era of heroism for the hero out of time.

Finding One's Home: Captain America Winter Soldier

Steve Rogers: Well, things aren't so bad. Food's a lot better,
we used to boil everything. No polio is good. Internet, so
helpful. I've been reading that a lot trying to catch up.
Sam Wilson: Marvin Gaye, 1972, *Trouble Man* soundtrack.
Everything you've missed jammed into one album.
Steve Rogers: I'll put it on the list.
[Steve gets his small notebook and pen out and notes it down
on his list which also includes I Love Lucy; Moon Landing;
Berlin Wall (Up + Down) Steve Jobs (Apple); Disco; Thai
Food; Star Wars/Trek (with Star Wars crossed out, indicating
that he has seen it); Nirvana (Band); Rocky (Rocky II?)]

Unlike the other superhero stories, this one begins with a new
friendship: Steve and an ordinary soldier. Unlike many, Sam
immediately understands Steve's difficulty adjusting:

Sam Wilson: It's your bed, right?
Steve Rogers: What's that?
Sam Wilson: Your bed, it's too soft. When I was over there I
sleep on the ground and used rock for pillows, like a
caveman. Now I'm home, lying in my bed, and It's like...
Steve Rogers: Lying on a marshmallow. I feel like I'm gonna
sink right to the floor.
[Sam smiles and nods his head]
Steve Rogers: How long?
Sam Wilson: Two tours. You must miss the good old days,
huh?

Steve certainly feels disassociated, emphasized by his list of foreign concepts in this new world. In *The Ultimates* comics, Steve has an equally rough time, as he complains about profanity in movies, hangs around in retirement homes with the remaining Howling Commandos, and otherwise emphasizes his status as relic of the past. While in *The Avengers*, he was quite grounded in the military with an arrogant playboy teammate and the world at stake from a supervillain – all familiar from his Golden Age adventures – this spy thriller is a truly modern tale, one in which Steve and his old-fashioned values don't fit. Nonetheless, his new friends aid him, giving him a place to belong.

"If we stay as survivors only without moving to thriving we limit ourselves and cut our energy to ourselves and our power in the world to less than half" (Estés 210). Sam agrees with this sentiment, as he runs a support group where he helps people readjust to life after the military. He insists it's all about dealing with the trauma:

> Sam Wilson: Some stuff you leave there, other stuff you bring back. It's our job to figure out how to carry it. Is it gonna be in a big suitcase or in a little man-purse? It's up to you.
> …
> Steve Rogers: Caught the last few minutes. It's pretty intense.
> Sam Wilson: Yeah, brother, we all got the same problems. Guilt, regret.
> Steve Rogers: You lose someone?
> Sam Wilson: My wingman, Riley. Fly in the night mission. A standard PJ rescue op, nothing we hadn't done a thousand times before, till RPG knock Riley's dumb ass out of the sky. Nothing I could do. It's like I was up there just to watch.
> Steve Rogers: I'm sorry.
> Sam Wilson: After that, I had really hard time finding a reason for being over there, you know?
> Steve Rogers: But you're happy now, back in the world?
> Sam Wilson: Hey, the number of people giving me orders is down to about zero. So, hell, yeah. You thinking about getting out?
> Steve Rogers: No. I don't know. To be honest, I don't know what I would do with myself if I did.
> Sam Wilson: Ultimate fighting? [Steve laughs] It's just a great idea off the top of my head. But seriously, you could do whatever you want to do. What makes you happy?
> Steve Rogers: I don't know.

Sam Wilson counsels Steve as the little voice inside him – the best friend of the future as the best friend of the past turns evil. Sam like Steve lost his best friend in war. Both have trouble readjusting to life in the U.S. and both have trauma to work through. However, Sam has quit the army, something Steve isn't sure whether to try. Chris Evans notes that the friendships of the movie were essential:

> Well, I think it's brought in more of a human direction. Cap's such a good guy, it's hard for him to bleed. Not just literally, but figuratively, you know what I mean? He doesn't want to burden anyone with his struggles, and unfortunately, that's what makes characters dynamic and interesting. So any way we can push him in more of a human direction where he does show weakness, and he does struggle, and he does connect with people and show vulnerability, I think that grounds him a little built. It just makes him more interesting. So all the relationships, especially with Natasha and with Sam. Even though we do have the Winter Soldier, he's more of like – we're doing third act stuff right now – so for the meat of the film, the majority of the film, the connections that he makes, I think, really bring him to life are with Natasha and Sam. (Keyes)

Cap was frozen in ice for decades, but in some ways he still is, as he refuses to date or find a calling or make a new life for himself. "In archetypal psychology to be cold is to be without feelings. ... While it is a self-protective mechanism, it is hard on the soul-psyche., for the soul does not respond to iciness, but rather warmth" (Estés 197). Natasha answers his withdrawal by turning gal pal, urging him to date and find connections, reminding him, "If you ask Kristen out, from Statistics, she'll probably say yes." As Steve goes on the run, she insists on joining him and breaking down his boundaries. She pretends they're engaged to throw off pursuit and makes Steve act like they're together. She's continuing to intrude on his distance, bit by bit:

Natasha Romanoff: Kiss me.
Steve Rogers: What?
Natasha Romanoff: Public displays of affection make people very uncomfortable.
Steve Rogers: Yes, they do.
[she quickly pulls down Steve's head and kisses him, making

Rumlow look away as he goes past them on the escalator]
Natasha Romanoff: You still uncomfortable?
Steve Rogers: It's not exactly the word I would use.

She ends the film asking Steve to call the "nurse" and Shield agent Sharon Carter (one wonders if the last name indicates she's Peggy's granddaughter). In a world that's falling apart, Natasha truly seems to have Cap's back. Chris Evans notes: "Her and I both have – our characters both have issues in this movie. It's just such an odd pairing. We're such different people. Her moral compass is for sale, and Steve is a boy scout. So it's interesting what they find in each other" (Keyes). She and Sam don't follow all the rules – they encourage Steve to question the new world around him and spark his rebellious instincts, ones that will be seen again in the Civil War arc.

Already torn out of time, Steve feels unsettled in a shifting climate, and this magnifies outward. First he discovers his unit has received different orders than he has, then that the World Security Council plans to spy on everyone, all the time. He and Nick Fury debate the difference between soldiering in World War II and forcing control in the present. Cap still has an old-school approach to trust, telling Fury, "Soldiers trust each other, that's what makes it an army. Not a bunch of guys running around and shooting guns." As it turns out, Fury has been hiding a deadly secret – a sky full of watch planes:

Nick Fury: After New York, I convinced the World Security Council we needed a quantum surgeon threat analysis. For once we're way ahead of the curve.
Steve Rogers: By holding a gun at everyone on Earth and calling it protection.
Nick Fury: You know, I read those SSR files. Greatest generation? You guys did some nasty stuff.
Steve Rogers: Yeah, we compromised. Sometimes in ways that made us not sleep so well. But we did it so the people could be free. This isn't freedom, this is fear.
Nick Fury: S.H.I.E.L.D. takes the world as it is, not as we'd like it to be. It's getting damn near past time for you to get with that program, Cap.
Steve Rogers: Don't hold your breath.

Morality was clearer in the past – heroes and villains, Nazis who wanted to conquer America and murder the minorities of the world. This time, however, it's Fury who plans to break the rules and Natasha who's betraying him, all with the best of intentions. Chris Evans notes:

> In this movie, I think the question is, well, what is right? I think it was a lot easier in the forties to know who the evil was. There's no disputing Nazis are bad. And now, it becomes a little bit more of a difficult answers. There's a lot more of a grey area. What is the right thing? And are you of service to that cause? That's where it becomes a tricky dispute for Cap because things were just done differently in the forties. Threats are different now, and precautionary measures are taken now, can be questionable and somewhat suspect in his eyes. So it's a tough hurdle for him to jump. (Keyes)

Obviously Steve Rogers is a man out of his proper time, but in his childhood he was equally the Ugly Duckling, small and gawky. Even his morality set him apart from the other children. The supersoldier experiment made him unique among his peers once more. Thus his trip to the future only exacerbates his sense of not fitting in. "When the culture narrowly defines what constitutes success or desirable perfection in anything ... then corresponding mandates to measure oneself against these criteria are introjected into the psyches of all members of that culture" (Estés 185). For Steve, this is the command to obey his superiors as Nick Fury spies from above and S.H.I.E.L.D. agents reveal secret agendas down on earth. "He is not entirely straight-laced either; he is spirited, emotional, and at times rebellious towards authority, in the true spirit of the traditional All-American hero" (Murray, "Propaganda" 139). Steve rebels and once more finds himself an Ugly Duckling and outcast in his world, the only S.H.I.E.L.D. agent in a building of Hydra. Chris Evans notes:

> It does have kind of a very grounded political thriller tone to it, and I think that just goes hand in hand with the character. It just works. And like I said earlier, they're also trying to infuse much more human conflict that doesn't necessarily have to do with fighting monsters and doing giant stunts. It's just about him coping with moral issues about right and wrong and good and bad. That's stuff we can all relate to. (Keyes)

In *The Ultimates* comic, the Chitauri invade the Triskelion,

71

disguised as S.H.I.E.L.D. Janet Pym, the Wasp, realizes what is happening and struggles to disarm their bomb big enough to destroy the solar system. Meanwhile, the Chitauri are successful in co-opting the psychics, luring S.H.I.E.L.D. into a trap, and slaughtering 20,000 troops. There's some echo of this as Steve struggles with the invasion from within. If the Triskelion is himself, the background soldiers within suddenly turn on him, forcing him to flee into the wilds of civilian America, discovering its malls and taking to the open road in a quest for safety. The outcast seeking belonging is "is symbolic of wild nature, which, when pressed into circumstances of little nurture, instinctively strives to continue no matter what" (Estés 185). Outside his comfort zone, Steve thrives and defeats the enemy at every attack...until he meets a force he truly can't handle.

Most disconcerting in all his struggles is his best friend, the one who knows him better than anyone, now returning as sworn enemy. The *Winter Soldier* plot is straight from the comic run of that name, of course. Black Widow doesn't appear, but the Falcon, Iron Man, and Nick Fury all aid in the quest. Cap's liaison to S.H.I.E.L.D. is his ex-girlfriend Agent 13, Sharon, as with the film. As the comic flashback reveals, the KGB secret projects revive Bucky from a frozen death only to discover he has no superserum and no memory. They give him a robotic arm and program him to be loyal to them – he can infiltrate America because he sounds and acts American. He began many assassination missions, all successful, and he is kept in suspended animation the rest of the time, even more split off from the world than Cap.

In the books, Bucky is Cap's sidekick. He lives in the training camp as everyone's kid brother after his career military father is killed, and soon becomes Cap's partner on adventures. As Cap is told in flashback, "Just like Captain America has symbolic value, an American teenager fighting alongside him... that's a powerful symbol too." Bucky has special training in assassination in contrast with the too-pure looking Cap. In the original comics, the pair have many adventures together. Then Bucky is caught on an exploding plane, unable to jump free, and a grief-struck Cap drives his plane into the water, only to return decades later.

When Cap of the film discovers the Winter Soldier, mysterious and famed assassin, is his best friend Bucky, he's devastated. His last bastion of security, his memory of a happy childhood, is

snatched away. He drops his shield (on many levels) and stands
frozen as enemy agents take him prisoner. Chris Evans notes:

> This was one of Steve's biggest sources of guilt, the fact that
> out of his whole crew of howling commandos were these guys
> that he convinced to come into battle with him. It's the one
> guy that didn't make it back, and that was the one guy that
> was always there for him. And then to find out that he did
> make it and was subject to some of the things he was subject
> to, that's a lot. That's a lot for Steve to process, and he takes
> full responsibility for it because he wouldn't do it any other
> way. (Keyes)

His sense of duty and loyalty to Fury manifest as Hill suddenly
arrives and saves Cap and his wounded teammates. She takes him
to Fury and they begin to regroup and plan in the sewers, the
basement of the mind where one can begin to heal and build a
stable foundation.

> Nick Fury: We have to assume everyone aboard those
> carriers is Hydra. We need to get pass them, insert the server
> blades, and maybe, just maybe, we can salvage what's left...
> Steve Rogers: We're not salvaging anything. We're not just
> taking down the carriers, Nick, we're taking down S.H.I.E.L.D.
> Nick Fury: S.H.I.E.L.D. had nothing to do with it.
> Steve Rogers: You gave me this mission, this is how it ends.
> S.H.I.E.L.D.'s been compromised, you've said so yourself.
> Hydra was right under your nose and nobody noticed.
> Nick Fury: Why do you think we're meeting in this cave? I
> noticed.
> Steve Rogers: And how many paid the price before you did?
> Nick Fury: Look, I didn't know about Barnes.
> Steve Rogers: Even if you have, would you have told me? Or
> would you have compartmentalized that too? S.H.I.E.L.D.,
> Hydra, it all goes.
> Maria Hill: He's right.
> [Fury looks at Natasha then Sam]
> Sam Wilson: Don't look at me. I do what he does, just slower.
> Nick Fury: Well... Looks like you're giving the orders now,
> Captain.

With his words, Cap demolishes S.H.I.E.L.D., choosing to
abandon the untrustworthy foundation of his life for a newer, far
more solid one. He's lost his army and calling without which he

thought he would have nothing. But he has morality on his side along with a small unit of friends and a quest to reclaim one more – Bucky.

Bucky is certainly Cap's evil twin and shadow. They're both augmented by higher-ups, and Bucky's boss Alexander Pierce even tells him: "Your work has been a gift to mankind. You shaped this century, and I need you to do it one more time." Similar things have been said of Cap. Of course, Bucky is important to Cap – enough to make the mission personal. Falcon notes in the comics, "Got you thinkin' you might have to put whatever's *left* of him out of its misery. No way that's *not* going to rip you up inside…make you question yourself in circles…"

The greatest difference between them is that the Winter Soldier is completely isolated. Cap however has always relied on close friends and beyond them the camaraderie and trust of the army. His first move as he infiltrates Hydra is to call on the agents of S.H.I.E.L.D. to defy the enemy among them. Cap's calling on the ordinary soldiers to ignore their commanding officers – sleeper agents – and defend their country is straight from *The Ultimates* (*Homeland Security*). As he ends his speech in the film, "I know I'm asking a lot, but the price of freedom is high, it always has been, and it's a price I'm willing to pay. And if I'm the only one, then so be it. But I'm willing to bet I'm not." Indeed, many agents rally to his cause.

Bucky and Cap meet on a bridge at last, symbolizing their tenuous connection. They fight as the Triskelion smashes, an interesting symbol. It's said that there are two sides to every conflict, with the truth as a third. Hydra and S.H.I.E.L.D., the giants are battling, but Steve protests that they're both forces of destruction and corruption. Both must end. They, along with the Triskelion are shattered, symbolizing Cap's old world, now blasted aside to make room for a better one.

Cap throws down his shield and Bucky realizes the truth, enough to save him in the end. Cap meanwhile turns his back on both giants to go after his best friend, with the loyalty he's always made a priority. In the comic, too, Cap throws aside his shield and Bucky realizes he knows the other man. There, Steve restores his memory with a cosmic cube, and Bucky is horrified by the deaths he's caused. He tries to smash the cube, and it and he both vanish, presumably to return another day.

On the film he flees, but takes the time to save Steve, indicating Bucky still exists within him. After, the world lies in ruins. S.H.I.E.L.D. and the Triskelion are gone, Steve has no job or home. Yet he refuses Nick Fury's offer of a position and sets out after Bucky, certain that by restoring his friendships he can restore the world. Sam Wilson pledges to remain beside him, reminding him that he's found a place at last. "When an individual's particular kind of soulfulness ... is surrounded by psychic acknowledgement and acceptance, that person feels life and power as never before" (Estés 183). Steve has a new grounding, one that will serve him well in the films to come.

THE AVENGERS FACE THEIR DARK SIDES

Abandoning Ego: Thor

As Stan recounts in *Origins of Marvel Comics*:

> But what was left to invent? Who could be stronger than the Hulk? Who could be smarter than Mr. Fantastic? We already had a kid who could fly, one who could walk on walls and ceilings, and a female who could fade away whenever danger threatened – or whenever the artist ran out of ink. As you can see, we were hooked on superlatives at that time, always trying to come up with characters who were bigger, better, stronger. However, we had painted ourselves into a corner. The only one who could top the heroes we already had would be Super-God, but I didn't think the world was quite ready for that concept just yet. So, it was back to the ol' drawing board.

Stan remembered a radio interview he had done in which the host had referred to the new Marvel stories as "twentieth-century mythology," comparing them to Greek and Norse mythology. With that, Stan had his great idea. Stan turned over the Thor concept to his brother Larry Lieber, who had been working on Marvel's monster comics, and had Jack Kirby do the art. After the first fourteen issues, the book was placed in the hands of Stan and Jack.

Norse myth is less known to a modern audience than, say, Greek or even Egyptian. Nonetheless, Thor's battles with dark elves in a world of castles and giant war hammers echoes popular fantasy, tying the superhero Thor seamlessly into recent franchise films like *Lord of the Rings* and *Harry Potter*. As with the films of Hercules and Perseus, Thor's film doesn't incorporate massive books of myth, but only a few characters and structures, leaving the creators free to play and create stories that focus more on special-effect battles than the world of the classics.

In the original comics, Thor first appears in *Journey into Mystery* #83 in 1962. Dr. Don Blake, vacationing in Norway, stumbles across an alien invasion from Saturn. Fleeing, he finds a "gnarled wooden stick – like an ancient cane." When he strikes it on a bolder, he transforms into man's greatest fantasy – a superpowered ancient god. Thus Thor, the mythic thunder god, takes form as Don's alter-ego, now clutching his mighty hammer, which reads, "Whosoever holds the hammer, if he be worthy, shall possess the power of Thor." Thor also discovers the hammer can control the weather and always returns to his hand after it's thrown. What's more, he can use it to fly. Thus he becomes a superhero. "He confirms the secret suspicion that even the disabled and the disrespected may one day turn into something far superior and far stronger than the prince of fairy tale lore" (Packer 90).

"In general, we can say superheroes reverse the usual order of '*persona*, outside, *shadow*, inside.' They turn the shadow inside out and show us the inside first" (Packer 135). The superhero is one's deepest wishes and secret desires – to be invulnerable, heroic, beloved. Thus crippled Don Blake reveals his inner god, the power buried deep within. His cane, without which he is "helpless" transforms into a deadly weapon and source of superpowers.

On beating the aliens then discovering he can transform again by striking his stick on the ground, Donald Blake returns to New York where he practices medicine from nine to five, then fights crime at night. His nurse, Jane Foster, is his romantic attachment. He has all the accoutrements of a superhero including a weakness – after losing his hammer for sixty seconds, he reverts to his frail human side.

This secret identity was more than a mask and cape – Thor used Shakespearean speech patterns and thought differently than his alter-ego. He knew all about Norse myth and secrets of the universe. It was finally revealed in *Thor* #159 that readers had it wrong the whole time – this wasn't Don Blake with a layer of Norse god pasted on top – this was the real thing. The actual Thor, alien-god of Asgard, was too prideful, so his father sent him to earth with amnesia to learn humility.

Despite this, Thor continues to live a double life, with his new love for earth and his beloved nurse. Thor finds new allies in Balder the Brave – Thor's loyal right-hand man – and in the deadly warrior Sif, Thor's intended bride. Eventually he adds Fabdral the

Dashing, Hogun the Grim, and Volstagg the Valiant.

Lee and Kirby, Thor's 1960s creators "were never reluctant to develop the humorous and even low-life side of Thor's character, which derives authentically from the Eddas. Thor is capable of being hoodwinked and outwitted. A quality which the Marvel Thor manages on some occasions to retain" (Reynolds 58). MCU Thor too always falls for Loki's tricks.

> The central conflict of the series involves Thor and his half-brother Loki, the god of mischief. Bitterly jealous of Thor and longing for Odin's throne, Loki unleashes evil scheme after evil scheme in efforts to either destroy Thor or discredit him in the eyes of Odin the All-Father. Some of Loki's plots even result in the creation of new foes for Thor to deal with, bruisers such as the Absorbing Man and the Wrecker, who reappear many times over the years. (Ryall and Tipton)

Thor's movie background is the inverse of his comic book alter-ego. Thor is a mighty prince with ono other identity, though in a nod to the old comics, Jane gives him a shirt labeled "Donald Blake" (whom Jane describes as her ex), and her team calls Thor this to rescue him from S.H.I.E.L.D.

In contrast with Don's humble origins, Heimdall introduces the film audience to his pantheon with a grand voiceover:

> In ages past, they looked to us as gods, for indeed so many times we saved them from calamity. We tried to show them how their world was but one of the Nine Realms of the Cosmos, linked to all others by the branches of Yggdrasil... the Worlds Tree. Nine Realms in a universe of wonder, beauty, and terror that they barely comprehended. But for all their thirst for knowledge, they let our lessons fall into myth and dreams. Where did he come from? He came from us, the proudest race of warriors the Worlds have ever seen.

We pull back to see Yggdrasil like a nebula twisted into the shape of a tree, permeating space. The film zooms in through the world tree to the capitol city of Asgard to Odin's palace. There Thor approaches his coronation in grandiose, theatrical fashion.

Also introduced is Thor's hammer: Mjolnir. As the film describes it: "Forged in the heart of a dying star, from the sacred metal of Uru. Only one may lift it. Only one is worthy. Who wields this hammer commands the lightning and the storm. Its power has no equal – as a weapon, to destroy, or as a tool, to build. It is a fit companion for a King." A hammer, especially this one, represents "the formative masculine force" the sovereign power of justice (Cooper 77). Immature Thor of course has not yet found these qualities within.

On the verge of his coronation, the conflict between Thor and his brother zooms to the forefront.

> Thor: Have you ever known me to be nervous?
> Loki: There was the time in Nornheim...
> Thor: That wasn't nerves, brother. It was the rage of battle. How else could I have fought my way through a hundred warriors and pulled us out alive?
> Loki: As I recall, I was the one who veiled us in smoke to ease our escape.
> Thor: Some do battle, others just do tricks.

When a servant laughs at this, Loki spitefully attacks him with an illusion of eels. Brothers often signify opposite qualities working as a team – "one figure represents the introvert, whose main strength lies in his powers of reflection, and the other is an extravert, a man of action who can accomplish great deeds" (Henderson 106). Here of course are the Norse brothers. While Thor has the public acclaim, Loki, the rejected one spends his life slinking in his older brother's shadow, until he resolves to take the glory Thor has always accepted as his right.

Of course, in superhero stories the all-too-public superhero self is the persona, iconic and larger than life, whom the public worship. "The interchangeability between *shadow* and *persona,* and secret self and super self adds to the allure of the superhero" (Packer 135). Thor has no secret identity, but his status is like a mask of duty and competence he's forced to wear – King of Asgard is an even greater role. Loki intensifies his conflict by disguising himself as Thor's friends and companions. In a shifting world, Thor is uncertain who to be.

Odin tries to crown him, with the words, "Responsibility, duty, honor. These are not merely virtues to which we must aspire. They are essential to every soldier and to every King." He has Thor swear an oath "to cast aside all selfish ambition and pledge yourself only to the good of all the Realms." In fact, Thor vows this but does not truly understand – he's never been deprived of anything. When Frost Giants suddenly attack, he's furious. Pride dictates his next words:

> Odin: And what action would you take?
> Thor: March into Jotunheim as you once did, teach them a lesson, break their spirits so they'll never dare try to cross our borders again!
> Odin: You're thinking only as a warrior!

Of course, Thor defies his father's orders and goes to challenge the Frost Giants. Thor's Warriors Three evoke different aspects of his personality: Hogun the Grim is a pessimist, Fandral the Dashing values glory as more of an optimist, and Volstagg loves gluttony and primitive impulses of the body. Sif cares much more for respect and duty as a proven woman warrior. Loki, added to the team, prides himself on offering "subtlety and sincerity, not brute strength" as the voice of cleverness. This group of friends represent parts of the self, but ones who are a bit detached, who can counsel and guide the hero. However, Thor wants none of their wise advice but charges into the Frost Giants' realm bluntly and challenges their king, who calls him "Nothing but a boy, trying to prove himself a man." When another Frost Giant calls him a princess, Thor eagerly charges into battle, swinging his hammer with a cocky grin. He dismissively calls the giants "ugly and stupid," while fighting with arrogant immaturity. Thor is on the verge of creating total war when Odin arrives to bail him out. Clearly a lesson must be learned.

> Thor: Whatever the cost, the world must know that the new King of Asgard will not be held in contempt.
> Odin: That's pride and vanity that talks! Not leadership! Have you forgotten everything I've taught you? What of a warrior's patience, cunning?
> Thor: While you wait and be patient, the Nine Realms laugh at us! The old ways are done. You'd stand giving speeches while Asgard falls!
> Odin: You're a vain, greedy, cruel boy!
> Thor: And you are an old man and a fool!
> Odin: A fool, yes! I was a fool to think you were ready.

Odin deprives him of his powers and banishes him. Campbell

notes:

> All these different mythologies give us the same essential quest. You leave the world that you're in and go into a depth or into a distance or up to a height. There you come to what was missing in your consciousness in the world you formerly inhabited. Then comes the problem either of staying with that, and letting the world drop off, or returning with that boon and trying to hold onto it as you move back into your social world again. That's not an easy thing to do. (190)

This is Thor's mission, as Odin sends him out to grow and learn to be a mortal, the most humble role of all.

On Earth, Thor initially continues to act as an arrogant, entitled prince. However, as he's knocked out by a small Taser and a nurse's sedative, he's beginning to learn. His new friends think him delusional (as do all the Avengers in *The Ultimates*), a serious blow to his pride. In both cases, he ultimately reveals the truth. Insanity can symbolize greatness, a level of perception not shared by anyone else. It is isolating, another lesson in humility, but it can lead to triumph once one is proved right.

Jane Foster, his guide, gets the task of civilizing Thor, teaching him not to hurl his cup at the local diner. She drives him to get his fallen hammer after S.H.I.E.L.D. agents commandeer all her research. Thor surmounts endless obstacles to get his hammer, the weapon that proclaims his mighty birthright and gives him his many powers. It is the outward symbol of his masculinity as well as his warrior might. But to his shock, it won't move under his hand – he's unworthy.

After, drinking with Jane's colleague, Thor says, "For the first time in my life, I have no idea what I'm supposed to do." This lack of certainty has finally crumbled his arrogance. When a drunk man in the bar taunts him and calls him a princess, Thor refuses to fight. Later he brings a new mug to the cafe owner and apologizes politely. Deprived of his powers, he's open to a new life without privilege. When his Norse friends come for him, symbolizing a new unity of purpose, they find him drying Jane's dishes.

> The hero may have to be brought back from his supernatural adventure by assistance from without. That is to say, the world may have to come and get him. For the bliss of the deep abode is not lightly abandoned in favor of the self-

scattering of the wakened state. ...Society is jealous of those who remain away from it, and will come knocking at the door. (Campbell 207)

If not for these friends, Thor might spend his days on earth forever, but they arrive to remind him of the larger world of duty and family beyond earth, the princely self he has set aside that he must reclaim – he is hero, not human. Nonetheless, his journey through another world has given him a soul.

While Thor of the comics maintains his secret identity on earth, the film version doesn't bother – he makes no effort to blend in and loudly proclaims his heritage. He is a prince and a Norse god (through *Avengers* and *Agents of S.H.I.E.L.D.*, awestruck characters keep emphasizing this), with no concept of hiding it. The original comics character is trapped in the usual secret identity conflict. When Thor reveals his dual identity as Donald Blake to Jane, there are reprisals. "He hath broken my law!" Odin proclaims. "My choice is clear! There must be a reckoning!" (*Journey into Mystery* #124). When his son returns to Asgard, Odin condemns him to "the ritual of steel," pitting all his guards against Thor, and ordering that "should he survive—he shall nevermore set foot upon the planet Earth!" (*Journey into Mystery* #125). When Thor wins the challenge, Odin confiscates half his strength and orders Jane to care for him, as he is banished (*Thor* #126.)

Much later, Thor returns to Asgard to save his people by defeating Seidring the Merciless. He collapses, and Odin is filled with remorse, admitting that he "hath judged thee too harshly," and "though I am said to be all-wise in all matter of things ... my wisdom fled when I turned against Thor ... my son!" (*Thor* #126.)

Likewise, when the frightening Destroyer invades in the film, Thor proves that he's changed:

Thor: I must stay and fight. I'm still a warrior, and I will fight by your side.
Volstagg: You're but a mortal now. You'll get yourself killed!
Fandral: Or one of us, trying to protect you.
Sif: The best thing you can do is get the mortals to safety and leave the battle to us.
Thor: You're right. Help me clear the streets. I'll let none of these people die this day.

He displays newfound responsibility for the innocents around him. When his friends fall in battle, he convinces them to leave, as he wouldn't be convinced earlier. He insists that he has "a plan," and approaches the Destroyer vehicle, humble and defenseless. He tells it: "Brother... for whatever I have done to wrong you, whatever I have done to lead you to do this, I am sorry. But these people have done nothing to you. They are innocents. Take my life, and know I will never return to Asgard."

The Destroyer smashes him across town. As Thor lies dying, having sacrificed his life for civilians, the hammer wakes. By proving his worth, his external power is restored to him. Once more he can don his divine persona and stride into battle, though now this divinity masks honor and goodness, not childishness. Clad in his full battle armor, holding Mjolnir in his hand, Thor is god of thunder once more, and tears apart the Destroyer. His rainbow bridge home restored, he offers an honorable truce to Coulson, if he returns Jane's research. The warrior prince has turned into one who will bargain and make alliances.

Thor's dark side is Loki, the rejected prince perpetually envious of his older brother, the glorified golden one. Listening to Loki weakens Thor and listening to his own arrogance gets him banished to earth until he can earn back his mighty hammer. On earth, Thor has to learn to listen and adapt in the ultimate "fish out of waater" situation. Only when Thor offers himself to appease Loki, giving what Loki has always wanted, can the pair begin to reconcile on a level below consciousness.

> Loki: You can't stop it. The Bifrost will build until it rips Jotunheim apart.
> Thor: Why have you done this?
> Loki: To do what Father never could. To destroy their kind forever. When he awakens, he'll see the wisdom of what I've done.
> Thor: He won't! You can't kill an entire race!
> Loki: What is this newfound love for the Frost Giants? You, who would have killed them all with your bare hands.
> Thor: I've changed.

Loki fights with his father's famous spear, but Thor now has moral certitude.

> Loki: Thor! Help me! Please!

Thor sees Loki is clinging to the side of the Bridge, looking up at him desperately. Thor reaches down to grab his brother's wrist, but his hand passes through Loki's. The real Loki materializes behind him and stabs him in the chest with Gugnir.
Loki: I was always more clever than you.
Thor: Yet still not clever enough.

Thor raises his hammer and summons lightning, striking each one of the Lokis. Battling Loki as his shadow has taught him cleverness, which he unleashes on his brother. When Thor wins and is welcomed on Asgard, Loki loses. Once again rejected, he rejects himself from existence and falls.

It is easy to look down on Loki for his years of trickery, deceit, and obnoxiously long and pointy horns. But unless we've shared his traumatic early childhood, how can we be so sure Loki is truly to blame for his evil deeds—and that we wouldn't do the same in his position, if we had his history and background? Looking at it the other way, how much of Thor's virtuous behavior is due to the fact that he was the favored son since birth, blessed with all of Odin's gifts? Is he truly good, or merely lucky? (White)

In *The Ultimates*, Loki tells Thor, "I was jealous, Thor. Jealous he sent *you* to save the world. I only wanted you to fail so that he might smile on *me* for once" (*Grand Theft America*). The sibling bond with its judgment and competitiveness significantly shapes the personality:

Because that permanence helps make it the safest relationship in which to express hostility and aggression (safer than with our parents because we are never so dependent on a sibling as we are in infancy –and in imagination always—on our mother and father), the bond between same-sex siblings is very likely the most stressful, volatile, ambivalent one we will ever know. (Downing 111)

Loki is all that is bratty and selfish within Thor, but also an inextricable part of the self.

Thor, unable to stop Loki's plan, destroys the rainbow bridge though he sacrifices seeing Jane again. Odin saves them both but Loki, filled with shame and regret, lets go and floats away. Like his comic alter-ego, Thor slowly learns compassion and wisdom from living with the humans. Nonetheless, he remains haunted by Loki, the dark voice from within screaming for acknowledgment.

Breaching the Underworld: Thor: The Dark World

Long before the birth of light there was darkness, and from that darkness came the Dark Elves. Millennia ago the most ruthless of their kind, Malekith, sought to transform our universe back into one of eternal night. Such evil was blossomed through the power of the aether, an ancient force of infinite destruction.

So Odin begins the film. The shadow of this story is the aether – a substance that's existed from the beginning of time. It cannot be destroyed, and having won the day, all the Asgardians can do with the aether is "Bury it deep somewhere, where nobody will find it." It's a force of power, so much so that "without it, the dark elves fell." Though the adversaries are vanquished, the aether lurks below reality and thought. This echoes the shadow, which can be buried but never truly eradicated.

Reynolds notes that "Thor has proved to be one of the most unusual creations in the history of comics: the first successful attempt to harness existing mythology on a large scale" to make a superhero (54). He suggests one reason for the popularity is all the inhabitants of Asgard being offered "in an accessible science fiction/fantasy style that linked them comfortably with the rest of the Marvel Universe" (54). More of Thor's worlds are seen in the film, with an epic *Lord of the Rings* style flavor for Asgard with castle-like architecture and a sense of history. There are epic battles with dark elves and giants. At the same time, space ships and space itself is carefully incorporated, with complex medical technology and forcefields. This all ties together on a surface level, in a way plodding, egocentric Hercules doesn't, as he often seems a god of his time when portrayed in comics. Unlike some stories, this one also finds a logical way to bring the endless wars between good and evil into the modern day. Mythology often features the realm of light and the realm of darkness. Each hero and heroine must travel from one to the other in the supreme ordeal, in order to spiritually grow.

On earth, nice girl Jane is trying to get on with her life and even dating. However, the aether removes Jane from reality and invades her. Touched by darkness, she begins her quest to the Otherworld seeking healing.

> In ancient matriarchal mythology, this descent was a desirable initiation made by female seekers of knowledge... The power of the ancient feminine would guide a woman down to the world of the unconscious, with untold wisdom as a reward. Even the figure of death was not menacing, but welcoming, as the immature anima sought her dark opposite. As the patriarchal Hellenistic religion took over, the woman's journey and archetypal eagerness for knowledge faded. From this shift in power came the legend of Persephone, an innocent flower princess who must be violently kidnapped to enter the realm of the dead. All eagerness to absorb the underworld's dark secrets vanishes, and a man drags the heroine on her ultimate initiation. (Frankel, *From Girl to Goddess* 124)

In this story, likewise, the heroine must be forced to the quest. This attack alerts a complacent Thor to come whisk her to Asgard, just as the police intervene. The nice girl of earth is suddenly a criminal, and moments later, a superheroine off on a magical adventure. Further, the aether protects her whenever guards try to remove her and insist her know her place as a woman who remains on earth and follows its laws. As such, it represents her unexplored shadow power lashing out, much like the Hulk's in his own story.

Their previous adventure had a clueless Thor wandering Anytown, USA. Now Jane, our human touchstone, embarks for the grand fantasy world of Asgard and the adventure of outer space. She meets the alien king and queen, wears Norse gowns, examines their technology. The final battle, though fought on earth, is in the "different world" of studious, proper Greenwich...with a massive black spaceship falling from the sky and many rules of physics inverted as the worlds converge. This is a magical realm indeed.

As the aether pervades her, Jane has visions of a red power overcoming Asgard. The Dark World too exists below thought, hated and rejected, but still existing. The dark elves, too long ignored, infiltrate Asgard and invade, beginning with the dungeon, a basement or subconscious realm below thought where another shadow, Loki, has been imprisoned. As the dark elves penetrate Asgard, Malekith, force of darkness, chases after Jane, seeking her power. His chosen warrior kills Lady Frigga, the loving mother and force of female dignity. The world of propriety, decorum, and law has been torn apart by the shadow.

Thor responds to Malekith's attack by deciding to no longer hide from the shadow but confront it, embarking on a hero-quest deep into its realm to save them all. Desperate, Thor frees Loki to guide them both to the Dark World, a place of cruelty and despair. In the Dark World, Jane's eyes flash black and she whispers Malekith's name. She senses the representative of the dark force that comes for her. He in turn tears the dark force from Jane as the worlds converge. She has a vision of him taking over earth with the new power inside him. He will shoot at the convergence of the nine worlds and destroy them all.

In Underworld tales, the hero famously must not partake of this place, particularly the food, or he will be trapped there forever. "The task is to pass through the land of the dead as a living creature, for that is how consciousness is made" (Estés 457). The taboo for Thor and Jane is the aether, which could make them one with the dark world forever and bind them to brutality, though it also offers immense power. In the underworld, they both pass the test and give up the power, though Malekith and Loki have different plans.

However, long before this the story is torn away from Jane, leaving Thor as the destined hero to fight the darkness, not ordinary Jane. She is relegated to the prize for which the men fight, or rather its container, as the aether exists within her. Jane's psychological development through the quest is thus cut short. She and Pepper in *Iron Man 3* receive superpowers, but each is considered an invasion or affliction to be cured, rather than a transformation to a higher state. Both end the story deprived of the powers. The conflict transfers from Jane's intensely spiritual internal quest to manage the darkness inside her to Thor's as he carries her around, taking the fight on himself:

> Thor: Let me take Jane away from here. Malekith is sure to follow, capture her and draw out the Aether from her. But in doing so, he will be vulnerable, and then I can defeat him!
> Odin: Malekith is sure to return, we have what we wants. And when he does, we will defeat him.
> Thor: We cannot fight an enemy we cannot locate! Malekith could be right over us now, and we'd never know! How many Asgardian lives must we sacrifice?
> Odin: *As many as is needed!* Till the last Asgardian falls, till the last drop of blood is shed!
> Thor: What makes you so different from Malekith, then?
> Odin: [mirthless laugh] The difference, my son, is that I will *win.*

Thor quarrels with Odin as the once benevolent king turns into a raging tyrant. An unreasonable and hide-bound Odin the All-Father appears in the comics as well. There he simply replies, "My law is the law supreme—and none may break it! Mine ears shall hear no more entreaties! Nor shall the voice of Odin mouth words of forgiveness! Thor has dared to pit his will against mine! For that, he must pay!" (*Thor* #126).

In the film, Thor must once more defy his father in the name of morality and his personal quest. The film now firmly transfers to Thor, who has external conflicts with the world's shadow, Malekith, and his personal shadow, Loki. Both will be settled in the most shallow of superhero conflicts – lots of bashing and smashing. Though Loki offers a trickle of self-knowledge and introspection, the film abandons its deeper journey.

There is only one path to the Dark World – through Loki and his knowledge. In myth, traveling to the underworld involves confronting the shadow, meeting it and learning all it has to offer. The Dark World is its realm. "In the topside world, all is interpreted in the light of simple gains and losses. In the underworld or other world, all is interpreted in the light of the mysteries of true sight, right action, and the development of becoming a person of intense inner strength and knowing" (Estés 449). Thor goes to Loki, and, as Loki's own shadow, breaks through Loki's facade.

Loki: Thor! After all this time now you come to visit me! Why?
Have you come to gloat? To mock?
Thor: Loki, enough! No more illusions.
[illusion fades, everything in sight is broken, Loki is sitting on
the ground looking devastated]
Loki: Now you see me, brother!

Same-sex siblings tend to be both shadow and ideal self for each other. As Jungian analyst Christine Downing puts it, "She is both what I would most aspire to be but feel I never can be and what I am most proud not to be but fearful of becoming" (111). While the pair don't trust each other, their dynamic has completely shaped who they are. They instantly understand the other's perspective, complete with fears and longings:

Loki: Did she suffer?
Thor: I did not come here to share our grief. Instead I offer
you the chance of a far richer sacrament...
Loki: Go on.
Thor: I know you seek vengeance as much as I do. You help
me escape Asgard, and I will grant it to you. Vengeance. And
afterward, this cell.
Loki: You must be truly desperate to come to me for help.
What makes you think you can trust me?
Thor: I don't. Mother did. You should know that when we
fought each other in the past, I did so with a glimmer of hope
that my brother was still in there somewhere. That hope no
longer exists to protect you. You betray me, and I will kill you.
Loki: Hm. When do we start?

Outside his cell, he shifts between illusions of Heimdall and Cap, taunting Thor with his honorable, trustworthy companions. He also transforms Thor into Lady Sif.

Loki: [turns Thor into Sif] Mmm, brother, you look ravishing!
Thor: It will not hurt any less when I kill you in this form.
Loki: Very well. Perhaps you prefer one of your new
companions, given that you seem to like them so much.
[turns into Captain America]
Loki: Oh, this is much better. Costume's a bit much... so tight.
But the confidence, I can feel the righteousness surging. Hey,
you wanna have a rousing discussion about truth, honor,
patriotism? God bless America...

Cap is Loki's complete inversion – a representative of truth and teamwork, the soldier who obeys orders. Loki of course fights only for himself. Yet confronted with Cap, Thor is unsettled. He's acting for honor and the greater good, he believes, but not as an obedient solider. Transforming him into Sif, another warrior who obeys orders to the point of death, is disquieting not because of gender, but because Thor is becoming someone else. In fact, Thor needs the criminal mind of Loki to succeed on their quest.

> Loki: You can at least furnish me with a weapon. My dagger, something!
> [Thor puts something in Loki's hands.]
> Loki: At last, a little common sense.
> [Thor handcuffs him]
> Thor: [grins] And I thought you liked tricks.

In many ways, he's developing a trace of Loki in his actions. Loki, of course, represents the irritating voice in the back of Thor's mind.

> Loki: You know this is wonderful! This a tremendous idea! Let's steal the biggest, most obvious ship in the universe and escape in that! Flying around the city, smash it into everything in sight and everyone will see it! It's brilliant Thor! It's truly brillian...
> [Thor hurls Loki out of the ship, and jumps out with Jane in his arms... into a skiff piloted by Fandral]
> Fandral: [laughing] I see your time in the dungeon has made you no less graceful, Loki!
> Loki: You lied to me! I'm impressed.

As they journey together, Thor shows traces of Loki, indicating that he's embracing the partnership with his dark side and learning by example.

At last they reach the Dark World, where alliances constantly shift. Loki appears to betray Thor, but this is prearranged. Nonetheless, there's believability in his words as he cried, "You really think I cared about Frigga? About anything? All I ever wanted was you and Odin dead at my feet." He gives up Jane for "A good seat to watch Asgard burn." All the while, he truly covets the aether, telling Jane, "What I could do with the power flowing through those veins..."

Thor retorts, "It would consume you." With added power, Loki, all impulse and greed, would never be satisfied, but devour all the universe and finally himself. The persona, external face of proper behavior – in this case Thor – must reign him in. In the underworld, Loki fulfils his role as shadow by offering uncomfortable truths: "This day, the next, a hundred years, it's nothing! It's a heartbeat. You'll never be ready. The only woman whose love you prized will be snatched from you." Thor and Jane's love is criticized by many, especially Odin the lawmaker, as impossible, but in this place of starkness, Thor must hear the truth. The raging force of greed within remarks, all too truthfully: "Satisfaction's not in my nature!" Thor can only fight against being parted from Jane, adding, "Surrender's not in mine!"

The pair battle each other through the adventure, as Thor notes, "I wish I could trust you," and Loki can only respond, "trust my rage."

Thor: [about Frigga] You had her tricks, but I had her trust!
Loki: Trust? Was that her last expression, trust? While you let her die?
Thor: What good were you in your cell?
Loki: Who put me there? *Who put me there?*
Thor: *You know damn well who! You know damn well!*
[pins Loki]
Thor: [lets go of Loki] She wouldn't want us to fight.
Loki: Well, she wouldn't exactly be shocked.

Though they continue struggling, each never trusting the other, Loki stabs a villain before he can kill Thor, sacrificing himself in a way that seems far more in character for heroic Thor than scheming, selfish Loki. It appears the partnership has rubbed off on Loki as well. In the Underworld, the hero often makes the ultimate sacrifice. Thor, however, loses the bratty selfish side of his personality rather than himself. Devastated by his brother's sacrifice, Thor clutches him in his arms, saying, "I'll tell father what you did here today" and offering him forgiveness at last.

"I didn't do it for him," Loki says, and apparently dies.

Thor battles the dark force with his hammer and it explodes, vanishing from view. However, the shards gather and invade the dark elves. Malekith, face half white and half black like Hel's, becomes one with the force. This is not a power Thor can contain himself, but one he must resist with all he is, there in the darkest of places. This only presages the ultimate battle to come.

By the climax, Malekith has turned completely black. He and his dark elves invade earth with the power of the aether and seek to destroy all the nine worlds. Their spaceships are black and red like monoliths of evil.

Clouds of red black dark force blast from him and swirl around him, emphasizing his fluid nature. He vanishes in and out, as Thor more straightforwardly charges, flies, and punches as the pair battle, finally alternating between Greenwich and the Dark World, they emphasize the two realms as sides of the same one, dark and light. Thor even ends up in the most prosaic world of all, the subway, which he must take three stops to rejoin the battle.

Their final battle is in a cloud of red. "Darkness returns, Asgardian. Have you come to witness the end of your universe…you think you can stop this? The ether cannot be destroyed."

"But you can," Thor retorts. The epic battle commences and Thor takes the villain apart with his hammer, which flashes white in bursts of pure heroism. As the villain is defeated, the worlds slide apart, finally separating as all returns to normal. The spaceship crashes down, nearly on a prone Thor, then on a prone Malekith in his own world, their identical postures emphasizing their mirroring.

Thor ends the story returning to Asgard to confront his father and tell him he's seen how power corrupts – he would rather be a good man than be king. Having experienced Loki's schemes, and faced the power of the aether in the Dark World, he rejects that part of himself and prefers not to use it as a tool to rule the universe.

> Odin: One son who doesn't want the throne, another who wanted it too much. Is this to be my legacy?
> Thor: Loki died with honor. I shall try to live the same. Let that be your legacy.
> Odin: I cannot give you my blessing, nor can I wish you good luck. … Go.
> [Thor offers up his hammer]
> Odin: It is yours, if you are worthy enough to wield it.
> Thor: I shall try to be. Thank you.

The throne is a destiny Thor does not want, but the hammer of heroism and protection for his people is part of himself.

After Thor departs, Loki reveals that he has been masquerading as Odin. "No... thank *you*," he says. Asgard has been left in his chaotic hands, with the apocalyptic battle of Ragnarok awaiting them in the future. While the underworld convinced Thor to reject ultimate power, it has only given Loki a taste for tyranny.

THE AVENGERS FACE THEIR DARK SIDES

Forming the Team: The Avengers

And there came a day, a day unlike any other, when Earth's mightiest heroes and heroines found themselves united against a common threat. On that day, the Avengers were born – to fight the foes no single superhero could withstand! Through the years, their roster has prospered, changing many times, but their glory has never been denied! Heed the call, then – for now the Avengers Assemble!"

Thus read the introduction to each comic. The Avengers are above all a mismatched team of outcasts: Captain America from Golden Age war propaganda comics, Iron Man, a science-based Silver Age hero of the early 1960's, the Hulk from 1950's monster comics, Thor from epic fantasy and myth, while Nick Fury and Black Widow represent Jim Steranko-era espionage comics and Hawkeye is an ordinary man. As writer-director Joss Whedon says:

The Avengers consist of a god, a supersoldier, a guy with a really wicked flying exoskeleton, a guy who's really good at shooting arrows and so on. If anything, the script came burdened with a Babel of clashing storylines from other movies, not to mention a raft of A-list actors who are used to being the center of attention: Robert Downey Jr., Scarlet Johansson, Mark Ruffalo, Samuel L. Jackson. (Grossman)

He adds in the forward to the first trade volume of *The Ultimates*, "Seriously, what are these guys doing together? This is a good idea for a team? With the Hulk? These people are together because the world needs saving. And this flawed, bizarre group of mismatched myths is the only team in the world that can save it and watching them do it is a glorious thing." As Stan Lee tells it in *Son of Origins of Marvel Comics:*

> "After kicking it around for awhile, we came up with what seemed like a perfect combo. We'd start with the Hulk, just to make it difficult. Then, we'd include Thor, 'cause there's always room for a god of thunder. Iron Man would be able to supply them all with weapons and bread whenever they needed it, and we'd toss in Ant-Man and the Wasp just for the sheer lunacy of it."

Of course, learning to work together drives the story as the characters battle their demons and each other as shadows. As Fury comments, "These people may be isolated, unbalanced even, but I believe with the right push they can be exactly what we need." How do neurotic, unbalanced people, each barely in control of their demons, become a team? That's the question *The Avengers* seeks to answer.

Thor has his own problems with the others, not only because his brother has endangered them all and he's ambivalent about their family connection. Thor believes Asgard is better equipped than Earth to manage the tesseract cube and Loki himself. When they refuse him, he grows hostile. Thus he, Iron Man and Cap battle in the forest. The woods, especially in fairytales, are the realm of the subconscious, where monsters and dark thoughts lurk, far from civilization. The three men all battle their own fears and insecurities in the other characters. All their emotions are heightened, to the point that Thor tries to kill Cap for attempting to break up the fight. Down in the subconscious, there is no veneer of civilization.

The characters all have internal conflicts of course. Captain America must master life in a new world. Tony Stark, his own boss, cannot work with a unit. Thor and Loki have murderous sibling rivalry. The Hulk especially learns to let out his rage rather than suppressing it or letting it control him. Natasha is tortured by the past as well as the co-opting of her partner Hawkeye.

Loki famously says, "How desperate are you? That you call on such lost creatures to defend you?" Each member of the group is damaged, coping with unstable powers and trauma or disconnect. However, in the first movie, they find their power as a unit.

Whedon explains:

> The problem is most of them have already been introduced. The real joy of most superhero movies is that origin story because it's that moment of "Oh, I have this power. I can do this. I can right this wrong, or stand up for someone." That glorious moment. I don't have that. These people have been introduced in the other movies. We may not know that much about them. Hawkeye basically had a few lines in "Thor," but there isn't anybody who's going to be like, "Gosh, what's this vat of radioactive acid doing here. Oh my gosh! I have superpowers!"
>
> That part of the story is gone. So what I've got is a bunch of more or less seasoned professionals: professional soldier, professional billionaire superhero, professional god. It's an oddly mature movie, and I don't just mean that it's thoughtful, though I hope that it is. It's about grown-ups. There's an adolescent nature to the origin story that these guys don't necessarily share. This is more about people who live in the world trying to deal with what they become, not about becoming it — except for the Avengers themselves, the team. It's the origin of a team. (Bercovici)

This final, most record-breaking film has the most superheroes, and consequently, the most conflicts. Tony is an instigator, pushing Banner several times to release his tight hold on his emotions, despite the chaos this would cause. "You're tiptoeing, big man. You need to strut," Tony says. He actually jabs Banner with a small electrical prod. Tony makes a fair point, that Banner cannot be a superhero if he never releases the Hulk. However, the Hulk is a weapon without direction. Whedon frames the problem pointedly: "The Hulk is a very hard character to make a movie about because he's not a superhero. He's a werewolf" (Grossman). The Hulk is divided against himself, much like the Avengers themselves. Thus he's the shadow of them all.

The Hulk is even stupider and less self-directed in *The Ultimates* comic. In the final battle, Steve Rogers must tell him that the supervillain slept with his girlfriend and the Chitauri pilots in the warships called him a sissy-boy. Both times, this is enough to goad the Hulk into action as he gullibly believes the accusations (even shrieking "Hulk Straight!" as he pulverizes the ships). He's also more brutal as he shouts his desires to attack his girlfriend and kill and eat Steve Rogers and Tony Stark in an earlier Hulk incident.

He actually does eat part of a Chitauri and kills 300 New York civilians before he's stopped. By the comic's end, there's no evidence that he's in control, or anything more than a terrible weapon that Steve has figured out how to aim.

While it's not addressed so directly in the film, Bruce Banner wanted to be Captain America, which is why he took the drug. As he notes in *The Ultimates,* "Skinny Steve Rogers enrolls in the super-soldier program and suddenly he's transformed into *The Living Legend of World War Two.* That's what I wanted" (*Gods and Monsters*). Cap became a hero and Bruce a monster, torn up inside with frustration at his rejection from society.

In *Indestructible Hulk: Agent of S.H.I.E.L.D.,* Maria Hill tells Tony that Bruce Banner has signed up to be a S.H.I.E.L.D. inventor and do good with his technology to balance out the Hulk. "I think Bruce Banner wants to be *you,*" she adds. In the post-credits of *Iron Man 3,* Tony is seen confiding in Bruce like a counselor, viewing him as a type of conscience. Thus the pair are linked, understanding each other on the level of science and creativity as well as their disabilities. Acting as the little voice of confidence within Banner, Tony tries to convince him to join.

> Bruce: I don't get a suit of armor. I'm exposed, like a nerve. It's a nightmare.
> Tony: You know, I've got a cluster of shrapnel, trying every second to crawl its way into my heart. (points at the mini-arc reactor in his chest) This stops it. This little circle of light. It's part of me now, not just armor. It's a... terrible privilege.
> Bruce: But you can control it.
> Tony: Because I learned how.

However, Tony plays with everyone's lives to make his point, one of the sources of Cap's frustration.

Captain America of course is an old-fashioned soldier who follows the rules

> Steve: We have orders, we should follow them.
> Tony: Following is not really my style.
> Steve: And you're all about style, aren't you?
> Tony: Of the people in this room, which one is; A. wearing a spangly outfit, and B. not of use?

Cap actually gave up his entire old identity to aid in the war effort. Thus he resents Tony's irreverence and total ego – the desire to have his name everywhere. Each is thus a shadow for the other. One critic sees the main conflict of the film as focusing on "the group's two spiritual opposites: Captain America, a.k.a. Steve Rogers, the earnest all-American square, and Iron Man, a.k.a. Tony Stark, the louche, ironic wiseass" (Grossman). Whedon adds that this is the tale of American values lost in the modern world: "We went from the world of Steve Rogers to the world of Tony Stark. I've described myself in this process as a Tony Stark who wishes he was Steve Rogers. That tension within me is going to be the tension between them" (Grossman).

> Steve: Big man in a suit of armor. Take that off, what are you?
> Tony: Genius, billionaire, playboy, philanthropist.
> Steve: I know guys with none of that worth ten of you. Yeah, I've seen the footage. The only thing you really fight for is yourself. You're not the guy to make the sacrifice play, to lay down on a wire and let the other guy crawl over you.
> Tony: I think I would just cut the wire.
> Steve: Always a way out... You know, you may not be a threat, but you better stop pretending to be a hero.
> Tony (that did it): A hero? Like you? You're a lab rat, Rogers. Everything special about you came out of a bottle!

Both are correct – the shadow knows how to push our buttons better than anyone.

"The qualities we have renounced and tried to root out still lurk within, operating in the shadow world of the unconscious," as Vogler puts it (71). Only by dragging them into daylight can the heroes understand themselves as full individuals. Joining with others in a family or partnership helps to complete the self – the differing personalities offer new slivers of completion.

The pair learn to work as a team with Tony relying on Cap to press a lever and save him, but this is born from necessity as their entire airship is going down. As Cap manages the task, despite being shot at, Tony takes out the shooter and saves Cap in turn. After, Tony is devastated by Coulson's loss.

> Tony: He was out of his league. He should have waited. He should have...
> Steve: Sometimes there isn't a way out, Tony.
> Tony: Right. How did that work for him?

Steve: Is this the first time you've lost a soldier?
Tony: *We are not soldiers!* I am not marching to Fury's fife!
Steve: Neither am I! He's got the same blood on his hands as
Loki does. Right now we've got to put that aside and get this
done.

Steve is the one to put this in perspective: Coulson volunteered his life for S.H.I.E.L.D. and gave it up in service, "doing his job." However, more important than time to mourn is the mission, saving the people of earth. Further, Steve is beginning to rebel against the system after Tony's provocation, while Tony is convinced by this argument and puts aside his ego to join the team. Their partnership is giving each shades of the other.

As additional baggage, Steve was the son Tony's father never had, the prodigy Howard Stark desperately focused his energy on and tried to rescue. Howard Stark says, "Project Rebirth was...he was the one thing I've done that brought good into this world" in *Agent Carter* (1.8). Thus successful Tony always felt like the second best son compared to perfect big brother Steve.

This of course brings us to Thor and Loki once again.

Rejected and cast from Asgard, Loki is determined to rule – if not his home, he will take earth for his kingdom and destroy it to hurt his too-perfect older brother, who has always had everything he wanted for himself. Thor, though betrayed repeatedly by Loki, still cares for him as a brother, protesting, "We were raised together, we played together, we fought together. Do you remember none of that?" Loki retorts that he was only allowed to live in the shadow of his brother's greatness, a role he's always resented. While Thor still doubts his brother will kill him (as evidenced by the look of hope on his face), Loki locks Thor in the Hulk's prison and sends it crashing out of the sky.

Critic Ensley F. Guffey describes *The Avengers* as a war movie with the moral certitude of World War II. "It is Stark and Rogers who carry the film's debate over why we fight, and circumstances force Stark to submerge his individualism, at least temporarily, for the good of the group and in order to achieve the objective, become a soldier, and successfully wage a war" (288). Loki is total tyranny, leaving the heroes to rebel against him. In fact, in his total power, he leads the Avengers to reflect on their roles: Tony must give up his superiority, Thor his pride and certainty, Cap his moral comfort. The Hulk must give up his control and trust his human side to guide the monster. In facing Thor, they all realize they've been larger than life and a team isn't about that but simple trust and friendship. It's Coulson, the everyman, who takes the bravest stand against Loki. Holding a superweapon, he mildly asks Loki to step away. "You like this? We started working on the prototype after you sent the Destroyer. Even I don't know what it does. Do you wanna find out?" Even after Loki stabs Coulson and he lies dying, Phil lectures Loki on how he "lacks conviction" and shoots him into the next room. A decent man doesn't fear the shadow and by facing it can break it to less harmful pieces. As he dies, Coulson points out to Fury that the others needed someone to avenge, or that presumably would have been his last word. In his memory, the team galvanize when Fury emphasizes that Coulson believed in them all.

In the comics, it's the public who are more skeptical than the heroes. Like Coulson, Banner decides to give them a goal. Banner deliberately transforms into the Hulk and rampages through New York. "I was only trying to *help*," he insists. "This was all part of the plan, you see. I was only trying to come up with a *menace* you could all get together and *fight...*" (*Super-Human*). His plan succeeds, though there is a death toll.

"We've never seen the Hulk build or create. He's never the architect of something good. He simply smashes and destroys" (Brewer 34). He's a force of annihilation, though sometimes this is what is needed, as in *The Avengers*. He's society's destruction embodied, though he lurks invisibly most of the time. "The Hulk has the Jungian trickster's ability to alter its shape so that it can merge with the human crowd, hence making it more difficult to track down (Iaccino 169). The Trickster's main function is to "bring about healthy change and transformation, often by drawing attention to the imbalance or absurdity of a stagnant psychological situation" as the natural enemy of the status quo, Vogler explains (77). Loki is a trickster, but the monstrous, rule-breaking Hulk is one as well. Thus he is the one best equipped to defeat Loki (gleefully slamming him about) and to destroy his ships as well.

In the original comic, *Avengers* #1, Loki begins exiled on the Isle of Silence, plotting revenge on the heroic brother who put him there. However, he has no interest in beating his human identity of Dr. Don Blake, but the real Thor, so he finds "a fearful menace to make the dull doctor become the mighty thunder god." This is once more the Hulk. Loki describes him as "the perfect foil for me," and makes it appear that the Hulk is running amok. The Teen Brigade rush to the rescue, but so do Thor, Ant Man and the Wasp, and Iron Man, who all offer their help. The Hulk hides for a time, but eventually gives in to Iron Man's persecution and they begin fighting in earnest. Thor goes after Loki with the words, "You were expecting me, Loki! That means you have committed some foul deed, knowing I would come to avenge it…And avenge it I shall!" Thor drags his brother to earth and breaks up the Iron-Man-Hulk fight. Meanwhile, tiny Ant Man and the Wasp trap Loki. The heroes then decide to work as a team with the Hulk reluctantly answering, "I'm sick of bein' hunted and hounded. I'd rather be with you than against you!" The Wasp names them the Avengers. Together, they form a team exemplifying balance:

> At the center of the core team is Captain America, the human, all-too-mortal touchstone for the team, and the group's natural leader, even when he's not officially serving as chairman (a rotating position that's decided by election). In the "heavy hitter" roles are Thor and Iron Man, who both add significant muscle to the team. While Thor's status as an Asgardian god lends the team a cachet of mythology and godhood, Iron Man provides the team's solid technological base. Hank Pym, whether he's Ant-Man, Giant Man or Yellowjacket, provides the team's hard science and analysis. On the other hand, his fragile mental state, troubled past and diminutive stature give the Avengers a touch of all-too-human vulnerability. The Wasp adds a lighthearted femininity to the team, and has grown over the years into one of the most capable and dependable members. The Vision's struggles toward humanity act as a reminder of just what the Avengers are fighting for, and his courtship and eventual marriage to the Scarlet Witch (who balances out the team's scientific emphasis with her sorcerous nature) gives the series some much-needed romance and a sense of family. Hawkeye's inclusion reinforces the fact that the Avengers aren't just a collection of gods and near-gods, but that a mere mortal with unerring skill and undeniable willpower can contribute to and even lead the team. (Ryall and Tipton)

In the film, Tony Stark and Loki are also shadows. This is emphasizes early as Loki takes over the German opera and invades in full costume with devastating powers where he postures to the crowd … then Tony invades, co-opting the speakers with AC DC, making a grander entrance from the sky, and beating and outclassing Loki. On the airship, Tony realizes Loki's plan because of how similar they are. As he says, "Loki's a full-tilt diva. He wants flowers, he wants parades, he wants a monument built in the skies with his name plastered...Sonofabitch!" Loki of course has taken over the Stark building, reclaiming Stark's patriarchal tower of power as his weapon to destroy the earth. Stark confronts him there, emphasizing his role as Loki's nemesis. He emphasizes that the Avengers, as a team, will come for Loki and adds the words he knows will hurt his adversary most:

> You're missing the point. There's no throne, there is no version of this, where you come out on top. Maybe your army comes and maybe it's too much for us, but it's all on you. Because if we can't protect the Earth, you can be damned well sure we'll avenge it.

Loki, master of protective illusions as Tony is master of protective technology, is usually untouchable. But without his suit, Tony emphasizes that Loki, through his attention-calling has left himself vulnerable. Loki uses his staff on Tony and it fails. While the story reason for this is Tony's replacement heart, on a deeper level, Tony's technological magic has beaten Loki's weapon. Tony is guarded against everything Loki might do, even being thrown off his own tower, as he does a midair suit change and the suit saves him.

When the Avengers reunite, it's as a real team. Tony abandons his superiority and tells Cap to give the orders. This he does: Hawkeye will keep watch for all of them, Iron Man will take the perimeter, Thor the invasion point, Hulk the enemy soldiers. Morrison says, "The Justice League was a Pantheon, the X-Men was a school, but the Avengers were a football team" (348). While each defends their zone, they work together, with Hawkeye advising Iron Man and Natasha discovering the flaw in Loki's interdimentional passage and asking the team when she should close it. Tony of course does make the "sacrifice play" after all, dragging the nuke sent by the World Security Council up to destroy the mothership and save them all. They've become a league of united heroes, even before they all enjoy shwarma together.

In *The Ultimates* comic, the Chitauri allied with the Axis powers and caused World War II, then rally to destroy the modern world. They Chitauri invade the Triskelion, disguised as S.H.I.E.L.D. It's not Tony's house, but in both cases, the enemy is threatening the world by bringing the battle to the Avengers' home. They also launch a fleet of warships, which Iron Man, Thor, and the Hulk battle. Comics Tony cannot disarm the Chitauri's bomb so insists they must take it far from earth. Natasha passionately thanks him for his heroic sacrifice only to be told with a smirk that of course Tony doesn't plan to sacrifice himself – only have Thor transport the bomb to another dimension with magic. The film allows Tony to truly put his life on the line instead of saving the world with a cheap trick.

In *The Ultimates*, one soldier gushes, "We were up against *spaceships* here. Fighting aliens who were in league with *the Nazis* for God's sake. It doesn't get more black-and white than that, right?"(*Homeland Security*). The film makes it even more black-and-white – evil Loki is starting an alien invasion and the Avengers must defend their hometown, civilians everywhere. "It was a story about broken people," Whedon explains. "It was a story about what we've lost that we used to have culturally, in terms of this sense of community, this sense of helping each other, this sense of self-sacrifice" (Grossman). Through the story arc, Tony comes to understand this.

The battles of *The Ultimates* end with Cap insisting they must become independent rather than working for the US government. Tony offers his home and his money, and the Avengers are in business. In the film they don't work for earth, but along with Nick Fury, they defy the orders of the World Security Council. *The Winter Soldier* and the upcoming *Civil War* especially emphasize that they can save the world, but not on behalf of a single government. This may have been an old fashioned war film, but darker days are coming, as Hydra is revealed as the parasite within S.H.I.E.L.D.

Performing Persona: Black Widow and Hawkeye

"Our personas represent the roles we play on the worldly stage; they are the masks we carry throughout this game of living in external reality" (Whitmont 14). All superheroes are persona as well as shadow. The world knows them as patriotic Captain America, mighty Iron Man, unerring Hawkeye. This is truest for Black Widow, a name with associations far beyond her character.

The Widow first appears as "Natalie Rushman," paralegal (and Fury's spy!) in *Iron Man 2*. In almost her first moment, she throws Tony's boxing instructor to the ground. However, along with her languages and paralegal training, she also has a past as a supermodel in Tokyo, complicating her feminine strength. As Tony objectifies her, pleading, "I want one," she instantly becomes his assistant, a sort of arm candy complete with revealing cleavage. After a scene changing in the backseat, complete with Happy Hogan staring at her (and by doing so, inviting male watchers to do likewise), she changes into a black catsuit, and shows off her amazing fighting skills. Perfectly controlled, not wasting a blow, she pulverizes a building full of guards, while the male chauffer comically defeats just one.

Despite her strength, her role as sexy star reassures viewers that she's less of a threat to men's power in superhero flicks. "That contemporary action heroine actresses are routinely drawn from the ranks of ex-models (Milla Jovovich, Rhone Mitra, Pamela Anderson, Natassia Malthe, etc.) or actresses known foremost as sex symbols (Halle Berry, Uma Thurman, Jennifer Garner, Kiera Knightly, etc.) ensures that any connotations of butchiness are offset by their status as undeniable feminine ideals" (Brown 203). Thus once more she balances femme and fatale.

Many critics have analyzed excessive femininity as performance, a way of reassuring the men by burying aggression, strength, and dominance in sweetness. Psychoanalyst Joan Riviére analyzes this type of disguise in her 1929 essay "Womanliness as Masquerade." She suggests flaunting exaggerated femininity in this manner is a type of mask adopted by women "to hide their possession of masculinity and to avert the reprisals expected if she were found to possess it" (38). Any strength must come through lipstick and seduction – this disguise grows so profound that it becomes a definition of femininity in itself. Natasha on *The Avengers* pretends to cry, gets tied up and acts helpless, wears a skintight bodysuit (to say nothing of her modeling shots on *Iron Man* 2). All this seems artificial, a way of captivating men as a Black Widow in truth.

The heroine who has had too much weight from society placed on her may have extreme difficulty finding herself among the too-strong persona or personas society demands. "Under each jacket is another jacket: the naked selfhood cannot be reached in the cold atmosphere of a mere reflected reality" (Whitmont 16). Natalia "Natasha" Alianovna Romanova has had many names and many identities, from ballerina to wife, agent, double agent and spy. She's had a myriad of costumes and lovers through her fifty-year history. As she slides through multiple roles in multiple films – a femme fatale, a soldier, Steve Rogers' confidante and fellow rebel, she emphasizes her flexibility. The truth behind the spy has not yet been revealed. The audience has never seen the real her, and it's possible Natasha hasn't either.

Black Widow first appeared as an *Iron Man* villain in *Tales of Suspense* #53 (1964), as the farthest thing possible from an action heroine. In a low-cut emerald dress with webbing over her cleavage, she charms Tony Stark on behalf of her Soviet masters. Literally everyone she encounters describes her as "beautiful." She's also a superficial character, as she happily dwells on Tony's good looks and wealth. She's easily distracted by a jewelry display in a shop. "Cunning and ruthless though she may be, Madame Natasha is a woman…and as such, she loves pretty things!" the caption announces (*Tales of Suspense* #53). She steals his antigravity gun until of course, he stops her. On a second encounter, her crocodile tears of repentance earn Tony's forgiveness.

She soon meets Hawkeye, a circus performer known as "The

World's Greatest Marksman" accused of theft, and running from the police. He plunges into her getaway car, sees her, and exclaims, "This is *one* dream I don't *ever* want to wake up from," while the caption describes "the daring, dazzling, dangerous *Black Widow!*" (*Tales of Suspense* #57). His desperate love for her makes him her willing pawn. He appears as an *Iron Man* villain once again in *Tales of Suspense* #60 and #64 (December 1964 and April 1965).

Black Widow, meanwhile, soon sheds her gown for a supersuit. Natasha's superiors decide, "Lady, you need a costume" and in *Tales of Suspense* #64 (1965), she wears a blue skintight suit with something of a fishnet pattern. With the new costume, complete with clinging boots and weaponized bracelets, her role changes – she's physically capable through her gadgetry rather than wheedling men into doing her bidding.

Once again, she charms Hawkeye into a partnership. She adds a mask to her own costume, imitating her subordinate rather than the reverse in confusing iconography. "All that remained was to design a *mask!* And I made one to resemble *yours*, Hawkeye...For *you* shall again be my partner!" she tells him (*Tales of Suspense* #64).

At last in *Avengers* #16 he returns, claiming to have been a misunderstood victim. "I come as a friend – not as an enemy!!" he insists. "I wish to *join* the Avengers." He explains that his love for "the beautiful Black Widow" led him into evil. He will always love her, but now her communist masters have captured her, and he has given up on saving her. As several Avengers are leaving, those who remain accept him, along with another set of former villains – Quicksilver and the Scarlet Witch. This is quite a shakeup for the saintly Avengers:

Hawkeye—well, he's an arrogant, hot-headed jerk too—and the Scarlet Witch, well, she has her own issues that we'll talk about later. (In contrast, Cap just died a few times, but he's better now.) Nonetheless, we should still be concerned about the fact that these three have performed evil deeds. A villain can't simply say, "Oh, uh, look, I've thought it over, and well, I'm a good guy now." Evil deeds don't disappear when one has a change of heart, nor do they vanish when just anybody says it's okay. In this case, it's appropriate that it was Iron Man who introduced the new Avengers lineup, because Hawkeye's entire criminal career basically consisted of trying to defeat him. So Iron Man has what contemporary philosopher Claudia Card calls the "moral power" to forgive

THE AVENGERS FACE THEIR DARK SIDES

Hawkeye: as a victim of Hawkeye's crimes, Shellhead has the authority to grant absolution and forgiveness. (Irwin 7)

His fitting onto the team is rocky – his flirtation with the Scarlet Witch annoys Quicksilver, while Hawkeye rebels against leader Captain America, thanks to his past problems with authority figures. Soon, his former mentor, the Swordsman, arrives. In shadow fashion, he is "The one man in all the world I used to fear," as Hawkeye says (#19). When he discovered his mentor was robbing the circus, he tried to shoot the sword from his hand – "In that moment, I became a man," Hawkeye adds. However, he failed and the Swordsman defeated him and left him for dead. The Swordsman decides he wishes to be the head of the Avengers and threatens to kill Captain America to make the new recruits, including Hawkeye, fall in line. He's acting on Hawkeye's sublimated desires, as the archer thinks, "Glamour pants is walkin' right into some kinda trap! But he asked for it!" However, Hawkeye and his friends work together to save Cap, just as Loki on the show makes them bond as a team.

Hawkeye's goal in the story is mastering isolation, as he begins *The Avengers* and his short appearance in *Thor* keeping watch from far above. It's his lack of connection with the others that leaves him open to persuasion. In fact, he's only close to Natasha, the one who uses their bond to save him.

Like the others, Hawkeye focuses on vengeance, though his is for himself, not for Coulson. He tells Natasha, "Well, if I put an arrow in Loki's eye socket, I'd sleep better I suppose." As with the original character, Hawkeye has gone from villain to Avenger, and as with his comic book alter-ego, the team quickly forgives him his past.

In the film of course he becomes a shadow of himself as Loki hypnotizes him into compliance. "You ever had someone take your brain and play? Pull you out and stuff something else in? Do you know what it's like to be unmade?" he asks Black Widow.

"You know I do," she replies. Neither character reveals a full backstory onscreen, though both hint at one that mirrors their history in the comics as partners working for evil. In the comics, Black Widow was the one to corrupt weak-willed Hawkeye. In the film she has a different backstory:

Loki: Is this love, Agent Romanoff?

110

Natasha: Love is for children. I owe him a debt.
Loki: Tell me.
Natasha: Before I worked for S.H.I.E.L.D., I uh...well, I made a name for myself. I have a very specific skillset. I didn't care who I used it for, or on. I got on S.H.I.E.L.D.'s radar in a bad way. Agent Barton was sent to kill me, he made a different call.

Natasha of course is a spy, best behind the scenes rather than in battle (perhaps that's why she's outmatched against the Hulk and Chitauri, and functions best when interrogating Loki or going in alone to turn Hawkeye back to the side of goodness). Clint asks Natasha, "You're a spy, not a soldier. Now you want to wade into a war. Why? What did Loki do to you?" Her only response is, "I've been compromised. I got red in my ledger. I'd like to wipe it out." She, like Hawkeye, killed decent people once and now intends to spend her life doing good, saving innocents in at least an attempt to battle the scales.

It certainly can be argued that being one of the smallest members of a superteam with grandiose powers is not the best use of her skills. Nonetheless, she suits up and heads into war. Black Widow's suit is tough black, popular with cosplayers for its powerful, sexy simplicity. While Black Widow in the sixties blended in as a spy in alluring gowns, the suit is more of a superhero costume. As such, it proclaims that the wearer is someone dangerous, with powers beyond those of ordinary mortals. In essence, wearing it makes her a superhero. She dons it in all three movies when she heads into battle. Scarlet Johanssen notes of the outfit:

It's totally empowering because once you get on the belt and the gloves and the bracelets and your guns and the boots, it looks great. It's bad-ass! And when I have my legs wrapped around some giant stunt guy's head, and feel totally ridiculous hanging on for dear life... it sells it. [The costume] totally sells things that would otherwise look absolutely absurd. It changes the way you stand; it changes your posture. You're more aware of your body, obviously. I think when you walk on the set everybody's like, yeah, it's the Widow: looks good. I've grown to love it. First, I was terrified of it; and now I embrace it because it embraces me, actually. (Blum)

She first dons the famed skintight black costume in Stan Lee's *The Amazing Spider-Man* #86 (July 1970). After an encounter with the Red Guardian, who is actually the Black Widow's husband whom she presumed was dead, she wants to make a change. She proclaims, "In order to *erase* every last *vestige* of that past...I'll begin by designing a new *costume* for myself." As she explains to herself, surprising readers by washing the black dye from her long, red hair, "I've got to become...the Black Widow once again. I've got to do what I do best...to fulfill my destiny...to help me forget...the haunted past!" She goes maskless, emphasizing that her face, like her costume, is an outward persona used to manipulate others.

In the next panel, Black Widow dons the tight black outfit, adding, "It may not be as fancy, but this new costume will be more in keeping with the swingy seventies! ... And with the modern image of the new Black Widow." As she also notes, her costume will "be the envy of my jet set crowd from Jackie on down!" It's powerful as well, sporting wristbands that shoot a "widow's line" wire for swinging, tear gas pellets, and a "widow's bite" electric stinger. She adds a golden chain belt to hold her "spare web-line" and "the powerlets for my widow's bite." She ends the comic by deciding, "I have my own unusual powers, my own style of combat, and my own strange destiny to fulfill! So whatever dangers lie ahead ... I'll face them my way ... as the *Black Widow*!"

"At the time, I think this elevated Black Widow to the level of icon," says Nathan Edmondson, the writer behind the current *Black Widow* ongoing series. "The suit was like an invitation, a uniform offered to the character as she was escorted into the halls of fame—or infamy, as the case may be. Comics are a medium—and isn't all of storytelling?—that is built upon iconography, and that means, for superheroes, a suit" (White). With a few changes through the year, the iconic black is the suit she wears today.

In her new outfit, Black Widow led her own series in *Amazing Adventures* #1 (1970), written by Gary Friedrich and drawn by John Buscema. Beside the Inhumans, Black Widow became the first female Marvel superhero with her own ongoing monthly series. "As the lead character in her own ongoing adventures, the Widow gained a level of competence and expertise rarely afforded to guest stars. She even gained a supporting cast of her own in Ivan, her confidant and driver. It's here in these issues that Black Widow goes from being a femme fatale to a force of nature by combining her new weapons with an updated and ferocious fighting style" (White). In *The Ultimates* comic, Hawkeye and Natasha dress identically in body-concealing black armor with long leather dusters, belts stuffed with spy-tech, and sunglasses. In *The Avengers*, both their outfits are more tight and revealing.

"When her amazing adventures came to an end after eight issues, Black Widow had irreversibly transformed into the powerhouse character we now see today in comics, cartoons, and films" (White). Unlike most of her contemporaries, who must be aged up or rebooted every decade, the Black Widow of the comics is seventy years old. As a young spy, she was given a drug to prevent her aging. Thus she is static, unaging as she watches the decades going by. On the film she lacks this augmentation. The computer identifies her as born in 1984 – either it is mistaken or she's far younger than her comic counterpart...though it's unclear why the KGB would program her in the 1990s.

Black Widow doesn't come out well in *Avengers*. She's good at interrogation, but against the superpowered Hulk, all she can do is run until Thor steps in to save her. She saves Hawkeye, but he is a normal human, the weakest Avenger of the bunch. In *The Ultimates* comic, by contrast, Natasha performs truly superhuman stunts, leaping from one building to another to snatch a rifle from midair. In *Iron Man 2* and *The Avengers*, she charms allies and enemies as apparently her greatest superpower.

By contrast, *Captain America: The Winter Soldier* sees her as a more competent spy. However, as she banters with Steve, he complains that she isn't trustworthy, as she's dishonest in every moment.

Natasha Romanoff: Nobody special, though?
[Steve chuckles]
Steve Rogers: Believe it or not, it's kind of hard to find someone with shared life experience.
Natasha Romanoff: Well, that's alright, you just make something up.
Steve Rogers: What, like you?
Natasha Romanoff: I don't know. The truth is a matter of circumstances, it's not all things to all people all the time. And neither am I.
Steve Rogers: That's a tough way to live.
Natasha Romanoff: It's a good way not to die, though.

> Steve Rogers: You know, it's kind of hard to trust someone when you don't know who that someone really is.
> Natasha Romanoff: Yeah. Who do you want me to be?
> Steve Rogers: How about a friend?
> [Natasha laughs softly]
> Natasha Romanoff: Well, there's a chance you might be in the wrong business, Rogers.

Her challenge here is sorting through her identity in a lifetime of lying and being lied to, using and being used. As she adds in the film, "When I first joined S.H.I.E.L.D., I thought it was going straight. But I guess I just traded in the KGB for Hydra. I thought I knew whose lies I was telling, but...I guess I can't tell the difference anymore."

She defeats Hydra by disabling their security protocols and dumping all their secrets onto the Internet. As a spy, she understands their weakest point. Their leader functions as her shadow – one with as much to lose as she has. Alexander Pierce tells her, "If you do this, none of your past is going to remain hidden." She hesitates for a telling moment, then continues.

> Alexander Pierce: Are you sure you're ready for the world to see you as you really are?
> Natasha Romanoff: Are you?

While she uses her spy powers, complete with disguise, to stop him, then punishes him with a spy's worst fear, discovery, she has much further to go. As shown through her conversation with Steve, she hasn't found real friends or lovers, only debts and allies. To form a meaningful relationship, she would have to share herself, a circumstance that seems quite unlikely. Until then, she will continue to wear her masks of badass fighter, costume-changing spy, and seductress, all artificial layers over whatever true self exists. She ends the movie noting, "I blew all my covers. I gotta go figure out a new one." It seems her masquerade will continue. Perhaps this shallow surface is the reason she hasn't been given a film, as writers can't find anything to latch onto, no vulnerability or truth. All they can do is have her strike down foes or change clothes.

As Scarlet Johanssen notes, "It would be wonderful to have the challenge of doing a female superhero movie where the protagonist didn't kind of rest on her feminine wiles and use every opportunity to strike a sexy pose in order to get the job done" (Blum). Kevin Feige describes her role in *Avengers 2*, saying: "We learn more about her past and learn more about where she came from and how she became in that film. The notion of exploring that even further in her own film would be great, and we have some development work with that" (Brew). Perhaps as the character continues to appear, viewers will discover what, if anything, lies below her perfect face.

VALERIE ESTELLE FRANKEL

Balancing the Anima: Guardians of the Galaxy

Peter Quill (Chris Pratt) wants to be a superhero but is just a "junker," a goofy collector listening to his tunes. Calling himself "Starlord, the legendary outlaw" only gets a laugh of course. The guard Rhomann Dey notes that the only person to call him that is "Himself, mostly" and that he's "Wanted mostly on charges of minor assault, public intoxication and fraud..." He's a connectionless space bum. Despite his alien knowledge and gadgets, he's still very human. "I think at this point he's definitely more informed by who he was on Earth," Pratt said about the character. "The arc of the character is a very human arc. It's really based on who he was and what was taken from him as a kid and something that he missed and lacks that he has to gain through the course of the movie, that's definitely what we're focusing on." The actor plays him like "Han Solo meets Marty McFly" (Perry).

In the comics, Star-Lord first appeared in *Marvel Preview* #4 (Jan. 1976). He's raised by a single mother, who's killed in an alien attack when he's eleven. Eventually he becomes a trainee NASA astronaut. When an alien called the Master of the Sun stops by, he offers the mantle of Star-Lord (an interplanetary policeman) to a worthy candidate. Quill volunteers, but is rejected in favor of a colleague he once treated badly. Undaunted, Quill steals a ship and takes his colleague's place. In the course of many adventures, he takes revenge on the alien who killed his mother and meets Emperor J'son of Spartax, who reveals that he is Peter's father.

In the film, Peter doesn't yet know this (though some of the audience suspect). Of course, the MCU likely plan to rewrite his backstory, as Spartax hasn't made an appearance. The Xandarians reveal that Peter's father is of an unknown ancient race and his mother thought the father resembled an angel. Characters already

117

seen who would fit this description include the Collector, Adam Warlock, the Inhumans from *Agents of S.H.I.E.L.D.* or Thanos, the ultimate Darth Vader patriarch. Even Loki would fit logically. Whatever the case, for the moment, Peter's adoptive father Yondu is his only family, and their relationship is terribly dysfunctional. Peter bursts out, "Oh will you shut up about that? God, twenty years you've been throwing that in my face. Like it's some great thing, 'not eating me.' Normal people don't even think about eating someone else, much less that person having to be grateful for it."

He's still hung up on his mother, as shown by his obsession with his beloved mix tape. It itself is frozen in time, containing only various songs released between 1967 and 1979. "That song belongs to me!" he insists when the prison impounder listens to it without his permission. "For most adults, if there was trouble with the mother once but there is no more, there is still a duplicate mother in the psyche who sounds, acts, responds the same as in early childhood" (Estés186). With his serious "mother issues," Peter finds many temporary love interests but no one long-term. His girls are reduced to jokes, from the girl he forgot was on his ship to the ones who have made it so filthy under blacklight. "In other words, he [must] find a way of freeing the psychic energy attached to the mother-son relationship, in order to achieve a more adult relation to women – and indeed to adult society as a whole" (Henderson 117-118).

Even his name "Star Lord," apparently was his mother's nickname for him, as she writes, "Dear Peter: I know this will be hard for you, but I'm going somewhere good and nice. But know this: I will always be with you, my angel from heaven, my prince... my Star-Lord." Of course, he cannot bear to read the letter or open the package, and keeps them unopened for decades, as if without reading, he won't have to say goodbye. He's frozen her in time and also his potential for relationships and emotional growth.

Jung saw the young man advancing through multiple anima figures – the soul-woman who appears in dreams and inspires the questor. First comes Eve, a figure of instinct like the tape that provides a soundtrack for his immature capers. Next comes a figure of allurement (Von Franz 195). Attracted to Gamora, he shares "I Fooled Around and Fell in Love" with her, nearly kissing her while she wears his headphones. This is a look into his world, a sharing of the tunes he had just insisted were only his. However, she pulls away moments later, crying, "No! I know what you're trying to do, Star-Lord! And I am not going to succumb to your... pelvic sorcery!" After, Peter begins listening to Gamora as an ethical and spiritual advisor instead of simply lusting after her. Her own struggles have given her a measure of wisdom and bedrock morality – vital for the young hero. As her actress, Zoe Saldana, says of the character, "Not only is she a warrior, she's an assassin and she's very lethal but what saves her is the same thing that can doom her. She has a sense of righteousness" (Perry). Her family issues are more blatantly addressed in the film: Gamora tangles with her adoptive father Thanos and especially her sister Nebula.

In the comics, her character first appeared in *Strange Tales* #180 (June 1975) and was created by Jim Starlin, When her entire species, the Zen-Whoberis, was destroyed, Thanos adopted her and transformed her into a weapon. In the comics, he did not kill her family, but vowed to avenge them. Nearly naked in a jumpsuit of two long strips of cloth, Gamora became so proficient at martial arts that she was called "the deadliest woman in the whole galaxy." When Thanos revealed himself as a threat to the galaxy, Gamora aided Captain Mar-Vell, Drax, and the Avengers against Thanos. Later, Thanos managed to obtain all the Infinity Gems, forming the Infinity Gauntlet (a device already seen in the Asgardian treasure room. With the Tesseract Cube acknowledged as an Infinity Gem, and another appearing in *Thor: The Dark World,* at least three are now in play in the MCU). At the story's conclusion, the Infinity Gems were divided among several guardians, known as the Infinity Watch. Gamora received one herself, giving her visions of the future. She joined the Guardians of the Galaxy in 2008.

Her adopted sister Nebula first appeared in *The Avengers* #257 (July 1985), written by Roger Stern. A brutal pirate-mercenary and cyborg, she claimed that Thanos had been her grandfather. When he took up the Infinity Gauntlet, Nebula managed to steal it from Thanos. Thus Thanos allied with various heroes, including Doctor Strange, the Silver Surfer, Thor, the Hulk, and Drax the Destroyer, to take her down. On another adventure, Nebula was one of Gamora's followers as they both battled Ronan the Accuser (*Annihilation: Ronan*).

"She is a Lieutenant of Ronan the Accuser," her actress, Karen Gillan reveals of the movie character. "And the daughter of

Thanos and sister of Gamora and they are on this Holy Mission to kind of cleanse the Galaxy of all that is weak, and that's kind of her ultimate objective and that's what's been drilled into her from when she was a kid. So she's kind of brainwashed by these people. She wants to impress and achieve and be as strong as possible. That's her ultimate goal" (Perry).

Onscreen, Thanos calls her "my favorite daughter, Gamora" in front of a glaring Nebula. She in turn says, "You disappoint me, sister. Of all our siblings, I hated you the least." While Gamora maintains her morality despite all of Thanos's training, Nebula gives in to genocide and celebrates it.

> Nebula: After Xandar, you're going to kill my father?
> Ronan: You dare to oppose me?
> Nebula: You see what he has turned me into? You kill him and I will help you destroy a thousand planets.

While Gamora resists her new nature, Nebula celebrates being nothing but a killing machine. She fires on her sister's ship, looting the orb from her body and leaving her to die in space.

> "It's complicated," Saldana said about their relationship. "I think to me that's the biggest heartbreak I guess for Gamora is the fact she wasn't able to save her sister. Gamora and Nebula have very, very similar paths. They were abducted from their families. Their parents were probably killed in front of them, so were Ronan's, but Gamora wants to change. She's just different. She's never really had it in her. I think that Nebula definitely was born with a sense of wanting to taste blood, so for her she doesn't want to move and that's something that's very frustrating for Gamora, because I guess there's this big responsibility that she feels to Nebula and Nebula doesn't see it that way, doesn't love her back in the same regard." (Perry)

Later, the two women battle. Once again, one of Gamora's new male companions must bail her out:

> Nebula: Gamora, you've always been weak! You stupid, traitorous...
> [Drax blasts Nebula]
> Drax the Destroyer: No one talks to my friends like that.

Certainly, having the powerful fighter (who's also a green space babe) always rescued by men weakens the character. However, it also hints at her own psychology. She cannot defeat her sister, her equal and opposite. Nebula represents a successful transformation into heartlessness – a cyborg in truth, stripped of compassion. To defeat her, Gamora needs the strength of friendship, must symbolically build up the male side of her own personality that can offer heroism (Peter), practical planning (Rocket), and defiant rage (Drax). Combining these forces, she escapes her father's control.

Little Rocket also has deep-seated issues, beginning the story by proclaiming he's unique. Yet later he breaks down, saying miserably of Drax: "He thinks I'm some stupid thing! He does! Well, I didn't ask to get made! I didn't ask to be torn apart and put back together over and over and turned into some little monster!" He begins to cry. Rocket of course has no family besides Groot, who is more of a partner. They are contrasting opposites like Sam and Frodo or more obviously, Han Solo and Chewbacca. Like the latter pair, the wordless one closer to nature is the voice of morality while the more human planner acts for self-preservation and practical payouts above all.

"I think Rocket is a great character and not just in a way that you would think," Chris Pratt revealed. "There's a lot of heart there. James did a great job of looking at Rocket as a real character rather than a cartoon character. So when you see the story unfold, you should feel bad for anything that was created out of nothing. There's a sense of loneliness and this inner pain that Rocket feels that hopefully the audience will empathize with that makes him a really sympathetic character but also so badass because he's a raccoon with a machine gun." (Perry)

"Rocket to me is really the heart of the movie," James Gunn adds. "He's this tortured little beast who's completely alone in the world … and yet he's still really funny. And so you need somebody who can do both sides of that" (Perry).

As explained in *The Incredible Hulk* #271 (May 1982), he and his first mate Wal Russ (a talking walrus) come from the colony Halfworld, created for the mentally ill (retconned in 2011 to a prison for the criminally insane), where the animal companions were genetically manipulated to serve as caretakers of the inmates.

THE AVENGERS FACE THEIR DARK SIDES

Thus it's unsurprising Rocket feels used and betrayed, designed to serve the needs of humans for his entire existence.

While Groot dates back to the horror comic *Tales to Astonish* #13 (November 1960), created by Stan Lee, Jack Kirby, and Dick Ayers, the character was an alien invader trying to capture humans for experimentation. He had a few appearances following, then in *Nick Fury's Howling Commandos* (2006), Gorilla-Man convinced him to join the good guys. "I think (Gamora) is intrigued by Groot," Zoe Saldana said. "At least I am. There's something about this. He's such a human and he's the most inhuman physically character out of all of this but he has this sense, this compassion" (Perry).

Drax the Destroyer has his own issues. With his family gone, all has been lost but vengeance. (In the comics, this plot parallels his film appearance, though he was once a human placed in an alien body.) He charges into death incarnate, summoning Ronan and his entire army so he can take that retribution, but of course he is defeated. Ronan's spiteful quip that he doesn't remember the wife or daughter and likely won't recall Drax himself is the final straw, and Drax is shattered.

After, Rocket chastises him for foolishness:

> Rocket Raccoon: [lands with his minepod on Knowhere next to Groot and Drax] Idiot, they're all idiots. Quill just got himself captured. [yelling at Drax] None of this would've happened if you hadn't tried to take on an frickin' army!
> Drax the Destroyer: You're right. I was a fool. All that anger. All that rage. It just covered my loss.
> [Drax shamefully looks onto the ground]
> Rocket Raccoon: [Rocket dumbly stares at Drax for a few seconds, then mocks him] "Aww, boo-hoo. My wife and child are dead."
> [Groot gasps.]
> Rocket Raccoon: I don't care if it's mean. Everybody's got dead people! But it makes no excuse to letting everyone else around get killed along the way!

Together, all these damaged, selfish, and immature teammates make up one whole person: Gamora's morality, Groot's quiet wisdom and compassion, Rocket's practicality, Drax's rage. Peter, the immature hero like Skye or Thor, learns from all these forces around him and transforms into a hero. Director James Gunn explains:

> "This is a story about a group of people who are finding out
> that they're not the pieces of shit that they think they are and
> it's really that simple. They all think they're pieces of shit at
> the beginning and throughout the movie they learn that
> maybe they're a little bit different than who they think they are.
> I think that's a nice thing to learn, and that's really what's it's
> about. So as long as it can keep it centered in those emotions
> and in those relationships, then I think the celestial head
> becomes a little bit easier to deal with." (Perry)

This growth is slow as Peter begins the story questing only for a payout. Midway through, he saves Gamora in completely selfless, even foolish heroism by plunging into space and giving her his own breathing mask, then quips, "I found something inside myself incredibly heroic...not to brag." While he insists on sounding self-deprecating and selfish, he truly cares for others:

> Rocket: Why would *you* wanna to save the galaxy?!
> Quill: 'Cause I'm one of the idiots who *lives* in it!

These unlikely companions are pushed together through common goals – they can sell Peter's mysterious orb to Gamora's buyer and split the bounty, while Drax tracks down his family's killer, Ronan. Thus they all escape prison together. An orb represents the lost feminine in Peter's life much like the Grail quest of Arthurian knights. Of course, he cannot access the orb, emphasizing the shallowness of his life. An orb represents eternity and dominion over the earth, the feminine realm (Cooper 74). When Ronan snatches the orb and they learn he will pervert it to murder millions on Xander, the heroes find a new purpose beyond a payout. Peter Quill, the central character and glue between these personalities, is the one to summon them to battle:

> Quill: I look around at us and you know what I
> see? Losers. [the others give him an off look] I mean like,
> folks who have lost stuff. And we have, man, we have, all of
> us. Homes, and our families, normal lives. And you think life
> takes more than it gives, but not today. Today it's giving us
> something. It is giving us a chance.
> Drax: To do what?

> Quill: ...To give a shit, for once, and not run away. I for one am not going to stand by and watch as Ronan wipes out billions of innocent lives.
> Rocket: Quill... Stopping Ronan... It's impossible - You're asking us to die.
> Quill: ...Yeah. I guess I am.
> [A pause]
> Gamora: [stands up] Quill, I have lived most of my life surrounded by my enemies. I will be grateful to die among my friends.
> Drax : [stands up] You're an honorable man, Quill. I will fight beside you. And in the end, I will see my wife and daughter again.
> Groot: [stands up] I am Groot.
> [they look expectantly at Rocket.]
> Rocket: [resigned sigh] Aww, what the hell, I don't got that long a lifespan anyway. [stands up] Well, now I'm standing. Happy? We're all standing now. Bunch of jackasses, standing in a circle.

Finishing off his hero's journey plot, Peter tangles with the genocidal tyrant of the galaxy. Ronan the Accuser, as played by Lee Pace, is built to intimidate. "He's the scariest thing I've ever seen," Gillan admitted. "Oh my God, he is so intimidating and also, he is really tall. He's just like one of the creepiest, scariest villains I've ever seen" (Perry). He parallels Darth Vader, complete with Death Star. His ship is the Dark Astor, a Star Destroyer-like ship with a double helix design. "It's big, foreboding, and awesome," producer Jonathan Schwartz notes. "It's about three miles long, it's massive. We're going to see quite a bit of it in this movie. It gets involved in a lot of cool action set pieces" (Perry).

Ronan the Accuser dates back to Stan Lee and Jack Kirby's *Fantastic Four* vol. 1 #65 (1967), then he played an important role in the *Kree-Skrull War* storyline in *Avengers* vol. 1 #88-97. When Earth became a prison planet, Ronan served as the warden of the planet, and he eventually became ruler of the Kree. His "Universal Weapon" transforms cosmic energy into disintegration or transmutation of matter as well as energy blasts and teleportation. As the Hammer represents patriarchal power of the sky, and the orb, feminine power of the earth, united, the two are omnipotent.

Though Ronan is the all-terrifying tyrant, Rocket slams a ship into him, Groot sacrifices himself to protect his friends, and Peter distracts him with a dance-off, long enough for Rocket to blast him. The heroes finally band together to hold the stone and wield its power against Ronan, destroying him. When they do this, they transform symbolically into a single hero, united in strength and purpose.

> Ronan: [horrified] You're mortals! How?!
> Quill: You said it yourself, bitch; We're the Guardians of the Galaxy.

At the point of death, Peter has a vision of his mother, and then Gamora takes his hand. Thus the feminine presence within himself offers salvation and completion. No longer an inner voice of instinct or seduction, Peter's inner woman has become a voice of true wisdom, guiding him to wholeness. "The mystical marriage with the queen goddess of the world represents the hero's total mastery of life; for the woman is life, the hero its master and knower" (Campbell 120). This is a moment of transcendence, one powerful enough to wrest the orb from Ronan and wield it with Peter's greater feminine understanding and intuition. After, he and Gamora find love and balance, and she reminds him that he has a family now. With the feminine restored within him, he gains the courage to read his mother's final letter and open her gift – Awesome Mix #2. Beside him are aggression, intelligence and nature, along with Gamora's morality and Peter's creativity – the perfect team. They head off into the heavens, a united band at last:

> Quill: What should we do next? Something good, or something bad, or a bit of both?
> Gamora: We'll follow your lead... Star-Lord.
> Quill: A bit of both!

THE AVENGERS FACE THEIR DARK SIDES

The MCU Shows

Traversing the Heroine's Journey: Agents of S.H.I.E.L.D.

Season one of *Agents of S.H.I.E.L.D.* offers bright, perky hopeful characters, most of whom hide nothing....at least through the tie in with *The Winter Soldier.* By season two, each character has shattered into a shadow or is otherwise forced to face it.

Coulson's death and return is the mystery of the first half of the season. As dark, vicious Raina and the Clairvoyant make him remember the knowledge buried within his mind, then he ventures into the secret base where he was revived, he reassembles the missing pieces of himself. The hero, on his epic journey, descends into the underworld – literally or metaphorically dying, to face his dark side. At the end of his journey, Coulson discovers another self-truth – that he was the one to experiment on people with a goal of saving lives even through terrible methods. Significantly, his own project has saved him, showing him reassembling the pieces of himself into wholeness. Only by completely surrendering to the unknown can the hero transcend his existence, and learn the wisdom and magic of mortality. He is no longer facing a midlife crisis, but an "after-life crisis."

As he grows through season two, a secret self emerges, scribbling alien words at night while May stands watchful with a gun. The text finally leaves them to an alien city and with the revelation Coulson finds a little peace. However, the alien voices remain within him, emphasizing a dark side waiting to emerge. As Gonzales protests:

> This is not a decision that we arrived at lightly. I know
> Coulson, he was a good agent. At least he was before Fury

injected him with alien DNA. Ever since, his behavior has grown increasingly more troubling. Can you honestly tell me that you don't share any of these concerns? ("Love in the Time of Hydra," 2.14)

Coulson admires Gonzales, describing him as "a brilliant tactician who has dedicated his life to S.H.I.E.L.D." Gonzales and his team are on the same side as Coulson but they don't trust him, just as Coulson no longer trusts himself. Being exposed to this splinter team makes Coulson reevaluate himself. "Maybe he has a point. I was dead, after all. I shouldn't even be here" ("After Life," 2.16). Their conflict continues through season two, representing Coulson's unease with himself and his new position as head of S.H.I.E.L.D.

Ward is the second to show his shadow self. One shadow appears early on, as the hypermasculine Ward's male aggression grows even stronger under external influence. In "The Well" (1.8), Coulson's team is tracking down pieces of an Asgardian Berserker staff. Professor Elliot Randolph (an Asgardian Berserker himself) describes the Berserkers to the team: "Berserkers battled like raging beasts, destroying everything in their path. A single Berserker had the strength of 20 warriors...Fighting with [the staff] put the warrior into a state of uncontrollable rage." Explaining the effects of touching the staff, Randolph tells Ward, "It shines a light into your dark places." After touching the staff, that usually-suppressed fury overtakes Ward, along with buried memories, all gifts of the shadow. He describes these to Coulson as "My worst memory. The first time I felt hate. And it won't go away. I don't trust myself." In fact, Ward yells at Fitz-Simmons and scolds Skye with misogynistic undertones:

Skye: The memory. Was it about your brother?
Ward: Drop it.
Skye: Ward, if you need to get it out, I am here.
Ward: Right. To talk. Because that's what you do, talk and talk. Don't you ever get tired of hearing your own voice?

The greater transformation comes midseason. With the tie in to *The Winter Soldier*, "Turn Turn Turn" (AS1.17), Ward suddenly shoots Agent Hand, the last bastion of honor in S.H.I.E.L.D. besides Coulson. "Hail Hydra," he notes, freeing his mentor the treacherous Garrett.

Evil Ward, admittedly far more interesting than his dull persona, reveals that everything that he's done has been a scam: "deep-cover tactics 101: perform selfless acts of bravery early on" (1.18). He infiltrates his old teammates at Providence Base, where he kills Eric Koenig, supervisor of Providence, and kidnaps Skye. Through season two, the "Evil Ward" or shadow persona runs wild. Unleashed for the first time since he was a teenager, the shadow stalks and kills Ward's brother. This brother, a senator, is the "good one" according to the world, but Grant forces Christian to confess that he is the real monster who tortured their third brother. The story leaves it ambiguous which of them is telling the truth.

While these character changes are significant, the greatest superhero origin story goes to Skye.

She begins the story as a trickster figure, unconvinced she wishes to join up. As she secretly works for her hacker blog, The Rising Tide, she breaks Coulson's rules. She always finds a way out, through lying and disguising, through charming villains in a bright pink dress in "The Asset" (1.3), using her gender as a tool.

> Quinn: It takes more than a pretty face to disarm me.
> Guard: Sir, we have a security breach.
> Skye: Oh, the timing on that was perfect.

"Postmodern female tricksters present a myriad of public personas, fluidly shifting between different impersonations as the situation dictates or destroying the old self to become a super-self" (Landay 11). In "T.R.A.C.K.S." (1.14), she plays Fitz's girlfriend. She also admits to cosplaying outside Stark Tower.

She has her own death and rebirth midway through season one as she's shot, and her friends resuscitate her with GH-325, a mysterious alien serum, adapted from the blood of a Kree. She revives to discover a new relationship with Ward but also a new assertiveness and caution.

Through it all, she seeks her origins, as she was once an 0-8-4, a mystery artifact considered the child of monsters and hidden for her own protection. Like classic heroes, she grows up with an uncaring foster family, or in her, case, a series of them. Through season one, evil Raina is her shadow, seeking Skye as Skye seeks herself. Though the women work for opposite sides, Raina too charms the men around her with lovely, harmless-looking dresses covered in flowers.

> Coulson: One thing before we start – what is it with the flowers?
> Raina: Who doesn't like flowers? ("The Magical Place," 1.11)

"Her association with flowers, beauty and the traditional feminine values marks her as an "assistant" rather than superpower in her own right. Eventually, her name is revealed as Raina, meaning queen…suggesting she's incomplete without her boss and king" (Frankel, Joss Whedon's Names 151). Thus she tries to appear sweet and seductive, hyper-feminine as performance. She flirts with Scorch, insisting that he has a wonderful gift and adding, "All I want is what you want – For you to be remembered, to be seen for what you're meant to be. A star" ("The Girl in the Flower Dress," 1.5).

Finally, both women descend to the innermost chamber with the mystery artifact, the Obelisk. Its mirrorlike surface suggests and transforms. The mirror is a sign for woman, not just in the modern icon of Venus.

> Rather than a sign of vanity, this mirror was a divine soul-catcher, or passage to the spirit world, as it was considered universally. … Celtic women were buried with their mirrors, as a gateway to the afterlife, and Buddhist and Christian teachings describe a future in which we can see beyond the shallow reflection of our current existence. Snow White's stepmother seeks her mirror's advice as from an oracle, and some magicians trap their victims as "slaves of the mirror" forever. In Egypt, the word for life and mirror is the same (*ankh*). One reflects the other. (Frankel, *From Girl to Goddess* 47-48)

In the same episode, she meets her father, Cal, who tells her the truth about her Inhuman mother. She finally has achieved her life goal, but sideways, as her father is all uncontrolled, raging shadow. He battles Coulson, Sky's "good father," emphasizing their role as opposite forces in her life. Calvin Zabo in the comics has an illegitimate daughter named Daisy Johnson. As is told in *Secret War: From the Files of Nick Fury #1*, the Hyde formula that made him a monster straight out of the classics gave her seismic powers, leading to her name Quake. Daisy eventually leads Nick Fury's team of Secret Warriors against the Skrulls and Hydra, and finally joins the Avengers. By receiving her new name, Daisy, Skye is metaphorically parting with the masculine sky and bonding with the feminine earth and its powers.

> Heaven is often the top of hierarchical religious structure, with the Sky God (like Odin and his son Thor) ruling over all. "Heaven is the universal symbol of superhuman power, which may be either well-intentioned or to be feared" (Chevalier and Gheerbrant 485). Thus Skye, in Buffy-like style, may turn out to be more powerful than the hierarchies of Norse pantheon and S.H.I.E.L.D. alike. This "single concept brings together meteorology, astronomy, astrology, theology, and notions of the origin of the cosmos" (Biedermann 167). Skye is thus all this embodied. While she began as a hacker, she learns self-defense from Ward, and other skills will continue to develop. Whether divided into the dichotomy of earth/sky or the four elements of alchemy and European medievalism, sky and air are masculine attributes. Whedon is no stranger to gender-flipping names and characteristics, especially with gentle Fitz and aggressive Melinda May. Skye may display more masculine attributes later on. Sky also often joins with earth in a mystical marriage. An "Earth" character is not evident, but may appear in a superhero with powers born from the ground below. (Frankel, *Joss Whedon's Names* 145)

After the transformation, Skye can cause earthquakes, an internal power, while Raina's exterior becomes monstrous. Both shed their sweet, nice girl personas, now revealed as killers and Inhuman. To Skye's surprise, her friends admire her: "You managed to be taken hostage by three known murderers, you gunned Ward down. Then were blasted by an alien chemical weapon and walked out unscathed," Bobbi tells her. "Leper? I think you're a rock star." Meanwhile, Fitz protects her secret. Her new, powerful shadow self, unleashed when she's frightened or angry, is beautiful and exciting.

The Inhumans, created by Jack Kirby and Stan Lee, were first introduced in 1965 in *Fantastic Four* #45. As related in "Who You Really Are" (2.12), the alien Kree performed experiments on early humans and prepared a small group to develop special abilities as Kree weapons. When this group encountered Terrigen Mist, they

could develop a variety of powers. Charles Soule, writer of
Inhumans, explains:

> They've been on Earth for 20,000 years and there's a lot of
> that history that we haven't ever seen. When they originally
> appeared in the Fantastic Four back in the early days they
> were already established in this very powerful hidden city
> of Attilan and ruled by a king and a queen and a long standing
> race with all this obscure tradition and history and all these
> amazing things that they've done that preexisted all the
> superheroes that we'd already been seeing in the Marvel
> Universe...The Inhumans have been having huge cosmic
> scale adventures for longer than human history's been
> around, so it's very fascinating. (Granshaw)

Skye not only gains a superhero identity from the Marvel
comics, but superhero abilities. According to Fitz and Simmons
she's the Hulk now – possibly a world savior but one who will
never be normal again.

> Fitz: Things change, that's what I'm saying, so maybe if you
> can learn to control this then you could have Avengers level
> powers. Something like Captain America even.
> Simmons: I think it best we keep in mind the unstable nature
> of Skye's power. If there is an Avenger equivalent right now,
> I'm afraid it's the Hulk.
> Fitz: Well, Hulk saved the world last I checked.
> "Love in the Time of Hydra" (2.14)

Meanwhile, another shadow emerges. Agent 33 (formerly
May's evil twin) wears a nanomask that transforms into Skye's
image. As Skye stands confused unable to know how to help
herself, she tellingly plays Operation, metaphorically longing to fix
herself. Her doppelganger arrives, like the lost part of Skye taking
form. Agent 33 cries helplessly and expresses how lost she is with
no one to guide her. As the evil version of Skye, she acts on Skye's
repressed and rejected desires and falls for Ward.

Lincoln, Skye's appointed mentor, shows Skye around "After
Life," the haven fellow Inhuman Gordon brings her to. Lincoln
emphasizes how she's safe and protected, brought to a shelter away
from the world where her powers can flourish and be nurtured. He
describes the descendants of the Inhumans as being "chosen,"

after grueling tests. This is a metaphor for growing up, transforming into the person she's always meant to become. At episode end, Skye's real mother takes Lincoln's place as mentor. She is a force of gentle serenity and wisdom, like a more powerful and gifted version of Skye's previous trainer, May. Raina, Skye's monstrous shadow, is in the haven, as well as her father. She hides in a dark cloak, unable to "bear the light of day," calling herself a monster.

> Skye: You got what you deserved.
> Raina: So did you...We're the same Skye....I am on the outside what you are on the inside. [She throws back her hood, revealing her monstrous face.] ("After Life," 2.16)

Raina however is locked away like an embarrassing secret to suffer and sob, while Skye is loved by her new parents and pampered like a princess. "I am *nothing* like her," Skye insists (2.16), but she's wrong. Surrounded by her parents and shadow-sister, Skye must face the darkness and light to grow through all these forces into wholeness.

Around her, the other characters also face their shadows and transform. Melinda May is best known for her one-sided conversations, in which she says nothing or next to it, and the other character offers all the dialogue. In "Repairs" (AS1.9), Skye compares May to a robot and says, "Target acquired: Threat eliminated." Amid conflicting stories, May's history is revealed in the same episode. She charged in, killed the enemy, and rescued twenty-eight agents on her own, earning the nickname "the Cavalry," but she failed to save a civilian.

> Skye: Did she lose anyone in there?
> Coulson: Herself.

In "Melinda" (2.17), this civilian is revealed to be a child, taken over by madness and powers she can't handle. May, before her change, is a happily married woman planning a family, kind enough to charge in and risk her life to rescue the girl. However, the evil child is a horrifying shadow of all her hopes, the monster child who kills and controls May's colleagues and then attempts to take over May. She kills the girl, who represents innocence turned twisted and evil. After. May is a shell, who transfers to a desk job, leaves her husband, and never has a child. All potential is cut off in the death of her innocence.

On the show, she appears all persona, masking extraordinary damage. Underneath her silence, she has a surprising light side, enjoying pranks and interrogating friendlies by offering them cookies. She shows passion as she seems to take pleasure in fighting Ward when he betrays her in "Yes Men" (1.15) and the finale. Her name is also a twist on expectations, as "Melinda" is British, and the combination "Melinda May" (admittedly as a first and middle name) suggests a name like "Betty Lou" straight from the countryside.

> Melinda May subverts this naming pattern completely: she is in fact not Middle American or eighteenth-century British, but Asian-American. Further, she is hardly the "girl next door" but instead a powerhouse of taciturn fighting skill. Her harmless-sounding name in contrast with her physical strength harkens notably back to Buffy the Vampire Slayer. Further, her names are alliterative like many characters in superhero fiction (Lois Lane, Lex Luthor, Peter Packer). She is the superhero of the plane, not just its pilot. (Frankel *Joss Whedon's Names* 147)

Further, her detachment conceals an overwhelming affection for Coulson: she creates his team, monitors him, and stays with him past the destruction of S.H.I.E.L.D., all to ensure he's all right.

May's coolness towards Skye also conceals respect and affection. With Coulson captured, May chooses her cruel words carefully and gets Skye booted off the bus so she can operate freely. In turn, Skye impersonates May with tight black leather and imposing sunglasses. This is one of the more blatant moments in which Skye trains at becoming May, looking to the powerful introverted woman as a role model. Near series end, May offers to help her train in "hate-fu" as Skye calls it – turning emotion into controlled power. Her moments as a spy are all revealed as benevolent, watching Coulson on behalf of Fury, and she remains a respected part of the team.

Bobbi, Hunter, and Mac all conceal an inverted personality as well. Bobbi, the ultimate loyal S.H.I.E.L.D. agent, is finally revealed as a traitor, spying on Coulson (who was duly appointed by S.H.I.E.L.D.'S head Fury) on behalf of a shadow S.H.I.E.L.D., the founders, led by Gonzales.

In the Hidden City, itself a shadow of the world above, Mac transforms from the friendly mechanic who resists being a field agent or indeed any kind of soldier. But below he is gigantic, bestial, ruthless as he preys on his friends. After episode ten, he returns, uncertain, with a temper that flares up unexpectedly. Within a few episodes, he's revealed as a traitor like Bobbi, conspiring with her against Coulson.

Hunter has spent his life as a lackadaisical mercenary, with no allegiance to anything beyond himself. However, when Bobbi attempts to recruit him, Hunter refuses definitively and escapes back to Coulson. It appears his disinterest is concealing a hero.

Season one's Jemma insists she's a good girl, so much so that breaking the rules make her feel nice. She's hopeless at breaking into classified information at the Hub, and impossible at lying. Seeing the handsome Trip leaves her clumsily blurting things, to her transparent embarrassment. All this changes after they lose Trip. Suddenly she becomes a crusader against Inhumans and all other superpowered people. It's likely this will lead her into darkness, as she's already pitted against her friend Skye.

Fitz's shadow is not emotional but physical. Ward is his foil through season one. On a mission in Peru to examine an 0-8-4, or "an object of unknown origin," Fitz protests Ward's heavy-handedness with sensitive technology:

> Fitz: Are you mental? I did explain in great detail exactly what I meant, using the Queen's bloody English!
> Ward: I use normal English—words like "duck" and "run" and "might blow us to pieces."
> Fitz: Oh. Oh! Well, congratulations, Agent Ward. You managed to string three words together in a sentence!

Fitz emphasizes that he represents intellect, while Ward is only muscle. Similarly, in "Seeds" (1.12), they trade comparable barbs:

> Fitz: Is Science and Technology what you imagined, Agent Ward?
> Ward: Yep. No uniforms, no rope course, no defined muscularity on anyone.
> Fitz: No marching in place, no I.Q.s in double digits...

In "FZZT" (1.6), Jemma becomes infected with an alien

disease and in desperation she throws herself out of the plane. While Fitz rushes after her with the antidote, the stronger more macho Ward is the one to snatch the cure and parachute from Fitz and jump out before he can to save the girl. In "The Hub" (1.7), it's brainy Fitz who protects himself and Ward on their mission, fixing the television for Russian mobsters and adapting the Overkill Device to save them both. He insists, "Before we left, you're not the only one that Coulson talked to, okay? He told me to take care of you too. And that's exactly what I'm gonna do." Later, Fitz gloats to Simmons: "I had Ward's back the whole time. Pretty much saved him from a gang of Russian mobsters and kicked a few guys' heads in."

Still, like a younger brother, Fitz insists that Ward would never hurt them and is still protesting this when Ward ejects Fitz and Simmons from the plane in a storage pod at the end of "Ragtag" (1.21), leaving them to drown. "Think about this! Ward, just turn around! Don't do it! Don't do it! Ward! Okay, you don't have to do this! Ward! You don't have to! You have a choice! Ward! Ward, look at me! I know that you care about us, Ward!"

Ward replies in stereotypical hypermasculine fashion: "You're right, I do. It's a weakness," and then releases the pod into the ocean. With hypermasculine Ward revealed as evil, Fitz is the one to take on the good, macho role. There is only oxygen for one, and he tells Simmons to take it.

> Simmons: Why would you make me do this? You're my best friend in the world!
> Fitz: Yeah, and you're more than that Jemma. [sighs] I couldn't find the courage to tell you. So, please let me show you.

He sacrifices himself for Jemma and sinks into near-death.

When he returns in season two, he's a shell of himself. The brain damage from oxygen depletion has transformed him from all brain with quips to match to the least articulate of the group. As he fumbles his way back, he proves more compassionate and flexible, less of an adherent to the strict rules along with the shattered and recreated S.H.I.E.L.D. Though he's lost some of his aptitude for technology, his heart is stronger than ever.

Assembling the Animus: Agent Carter

Set in 1946 New York, the pilot establishes Agent Carter's connection to Captain Rogers then launches into a post-war story of espionage. Peggy works for a clandestine and patriotic organization (SSR) where she is often treated like most secretaries in the forties.

Peggy begins her own series devastated at losing Steve Rogers. As Jarvis tells her early on, "From what Mr. Stark has told me, Captain Rodgers relied heavily on you. For courage, strategy, and moral guidance. You were his support. Your desire to help others is noble, but I doubt you'll find much success unless you allow others to help you" ("Bridge and Tunnel" 1.2). Thus she searches for a new mission and team without the certainty of war or her love for Steve.

This confusion and displacement was common for women in the post-war years.

> Riveters built planes and the Women Airforce Service Pilots (WASPs) flew them. Women were nurses overseas and ballplayers at home. For the first time, they were not only *allowed* into exciting new positions in the public sphere, but were actually *encouraged* by those in power to be there. (Stuller 19)

Peggy's confusion is reflected in her myriad of secret identities. Unlike the superhero men of the franchise, Peggy Carter's life is lies and manipulations. She is a proper young telephone receptionist for those she keeps at a distance, including her roommate and her landlady. The SSR men only give her lunch orders and filing. She uses these many personas as camouflage as she undertakes a spy mission for Howard Stark:

Granted, she knows the SSR men regard her as little better

than a secretary and she flips this disadvantage into a disguise. She fetches coffee in order to spy on the men's meeting and requests a sick day because of "ladies things" – her disgusted boss hastily tells her to go shopping or do whatever she likes. She arms herself with staplers, stoves, and perfume bottles and turns the innocuous tools of a woman's world into weapons. But when even her lie about Howard Stark to throw investigators off the trail involves him kissing her on VE Day, one must ask if she must act seductive or frail in every scene with her fellow agents.

Later, her milk inspector costume is meant to be geeky and forgettable, with glasses and tightly-bunned hair. In "Now is Not the End" (1.1), she disguises as a sexy blonde bombshell in a low-cut silver gown, an attractive femme fatale who's the shadow of herself. This costume is designed to seduce, but as an equally forgettable mystery woman. Thus dressed, she charms club owner and fence Spider Raymond then kisses him, knocking him out with her potent lipstick. Peggy slinks into her adversary's office, and with lines delivered in a lush bedroom voice like "I hope you don't find me forward" and "let's make this a game" she sits on his lap and kisses him. This of course represents her sexuality turned weapon. On her way out she grabs a man and dance with him, as a distraction, and of course, he's happy to oblige such a sultry femme fatale. Even her milk inspector outfit has a trace of this, as she procures it from a closet in Howard Stark's bedroom, meant for his "theatrical" games.

Her statement-making red hat appears in one scene then vanishes back into the closet, much like the statement-making character herself. Peggy's room has drawers of pink sweaters and embroidered handkerchiefs, but underneath is a hidden drawer with her intel from Stark.

> Mr. Jones: I didn't know our government had such good taste in secretaries. What's your name darling?
> Peggy: Agent.
> Mr. Jones: That has a lovely ring to it. (1.1)

Certainly, Peggy Carter gets some zingers in when the men insult her. When asked to file because she's "so good with that sort of thing" (a backhanded compliment suggesting she's *not* good at investigation or "real work"), she responds: "What kind of thing is that, Agent Thompson, the alphabet? I can teach you. Let's start with words beginning with 'A.'" She clobbers a fleeing villain with a briefcase then politely offers her less competent colleague more help if he needs it. As she spends the rest of her SSR time sneaking about and claiming women's troubles, she's not living up to her one-liners…at least not in public.

In the office she comes to care for Daniel Sousa, who is marginalized for his lost leg as she is for her gender. He has more perception than the other men, especially about Peggy and her new mission. Even the clods in her office teach her about life in her era, as she notes, "I can trust the actions of men who don't respect me more than those who do. At least when they ask for something, they mean it" (1.4). Nonetheless, she learns to work with all of them, even the bitter Agent Thomson.

Just as the anima represents man's inner feminine, the animus is woman's inner masculine. This animus "evokes masculine traits within her: logic, rationality, intellect. Her conscious side, aware of the world around her, grows, and she can rule and comprehend the exterior world" (Frankel, *From Girl to Goddess* 22). With these friends around her, Peggy's psyche grows. At the most superficial level, the animus is a force of brute strength and power like the thugs she fights or the office misogynistic cavemen who know how to interrogate. As the heroine grows, her animus matures, or is replaced by a wiser animus when she's ready for his more developed stages: initiative and planning, rule of law, and wisdom. The planning side soon appears as the heroine sets out on her quest (Von Franz 206).

This is Howard Stark, the bad boy as Steve Rogers was the good one. When he tricks her into getting Steve's blood back for him from SSR, she finally unloads about what she thinks of him:

> I think you're a man out for his own gain no matter who you're charging. You are constantly finding holes to slither your way into in the hope of finding loose change, only to cry when you're bitten by another snake. You're a man who says "I love you" whilst looking over a woman's shoulder into the mirror. Steve Rogers dedicated his mind, his body, his life to the SSR and to this country, not to your bank account. I made the same pledge, but I'm not as good as Steve was. I forgot my pledge running around for you like a corporate spy. So thank you, Howard, for reminding me who Steve was and what I aspire to be. ("The Blitzkrieg Button," 1.4)

At the same time, they're both obsessed with finding Steve Rogers, the man both of them led to his death.

Most important to the story is her partner Jarvis. He represents the third stage of animus wisdom, judgment and the law. He also embodies truth, emphasized in his inability to lie. Unlike emotional, action-powered Carter, Jarvis is completely steady:

> Agent Peggy Carter: The next time you approach a woman in a dark alley, you might want to introduce yourself.
> Edwin Jarvis: Well, I shall endeavor to remember that, provided my concussion isn't too severe. Should you need me, call any time before 9:00.
> Agent Peggy Carter: What happens at 9:00?
> Edwin Jarvis: My wife and I go to bed. 7:00, sherry, 8:00, Benny Goodman. 9:00, bed.
> Agent Peggy Carter: You're new to espionage, aren't you?
> Edwin Jarvis: Far from it. Last summer, I caught the cook pocketing the good spoons. What now, Miss Carter?
> Agent Peggy Carter: Now I go to work. (1.1)

Carter's greatest problem is her colleagues and their dismissal of her skills. In the film *Captain America*, she goes into combat at Red Skull's headquarters, gun in hand (though this was rare to impossible for the American army). However, the post-war world wanted women back in their homes so men could reclaim their jobs. Carter is barred from the mission to Russia, even after translating the code no one else can and pointing out, "There's no one more qualified for this mission sir. I *am* going to Russia. ("The Iron Ceiling," 1.5). She only gets added when she recruits the Howling Commandos. On the mission under the inexperienced Agent Thompson, she has better tactical skills and soon claims command. He meanwhile crouches frozen in the corner as, under heavy fire, she continues giving orders. "Not bad for a girl," says Dr. Ivchenko, the scientist they've freed. Back home, finally caught for spying, Carter tells her coworkers why she's gone independent:

> Roger Dooley: I'm supposed to believe that you pulled off your own investigation without any of us noticing?
> Daniel Sousa: Now, why would you go through all that trouble instead of coming to one of us?
> Peggy Carter: I conducted my own investigation because no

one listens to me. I got away with it because no one looks at me. Because, unless I have your reports, your coffee, or your lunch, I'm invisible. ("SNAFU," 1.7)

Though she's operating in man's world, she has female friends like her dead roommate Colleen and waitress neighbor Angie (female companions who often are left out of similar stories). They are her shadows – women as normal as she pretends to be but cannot truly manage.

Another shadow appears as the helpless damsel "Betty Carver" of fictional Captain America adventures. "If only Captain America were here to rescue me," the flimsy radio heroine cries as Carter beats up a villain without a man's help. This clear juxtaposition emphasizes how Carter plans to take the place of Captain America, not the damsel in distress. Their touching goodbye is reenacted on the radio play in the final episode, emphasizing the goodbye the real Carter finally manages to make.

Of course, this shadow in fact foreshadows the real shadow who comes. While Peggy's accent and gender mark her as "other" wherever she goes, Dorothy "Dottie" Underwood from provincial American Iowa appears to fit right into the all-women's community. Carter faces her dark side as the evil Russian assassin, while she, in traditional superheroine fashion, is the protector of life. They are set from the start as hero and villain:

> Peggy Carter: If you want to get to know New York – if you want to get know any place, you have to start with the people first.
> Dottie Underwood: I talk to people.
> Peggy Carter: Real people with real jobs. Not the, uh, phony, superficial ones that pervade the city. Uh, you should start with Brooklyn first.
> Dottie Underwood: But I-I'd rather see the Statue of Liberty.
> Peggy Carter: Oh, she'll still be there. But what she represents, the spirit of Lady Liberty, is found in its people.
> Dottie Underwood: Wow. You sounded like Captain America just now.
> Peggy Carter: That's not a bad thing. ("The Iron Ceiling," 1.5).

Dottie dreams of snapping the neck of a childhood friend who gave her a half a roll...then she offers half of hers to Peggy over breakfast, foreshadowing her plans (1.5). Soon, Dottie steals

Peggy's knockout lipstick and uses it to kiss Peggy, turning her own weapon on her in "A Sin to Err" (1.6). She charms men as Peggy does, though she then kills them.

The women spar in business suits in the final episode, Peggy in blue and white, Dottie in black and red. Dottie emphasizes their connection – Peggy as the good girl and Dottie as the disguised ignored half, the little girl locked away. "I used to be so jealous of girls like you. I would've done anything to walk like you, to talk like you. But now I can be anybody I want. Oh I've got a great idea! Maybe I'll be an SSR agent next. Whaddya think of that?" They stand facing each other and Dottie adds, "I thought you'd be better."

While the women have their showdown, Dr. Ivchenko beguiles Stark, pushing him with his guilt over Captain America – the same guilt Peggy has felt all this time. He uses his voice as his power, and hypnotizes Stark into poisoning everyone in Times Square on V.E. Day. Peggy must counter with better persuasion – the power of truth. "Howard, Steve is gone. He died over a year ago…this won't bring him back…Steve is gone. We have to move on, all of us. As impossible as this may sound, we have to bring him home." Her words reach Stark as well as the guilt-ridden part of herself. He turns the plane around and New York is saved. By counseling him, while keeping the memory of Steve tucked within, she has achieved the final animus stage – wisdom. "The positive side of the animus can personify an enterprising spirit, courage, truthfulness, and the highest form, spiritual profundity. Through him, a woman can experience the underlying processes of her cultural and personal objective situation and can find her way to an intensified spiritual attitude to life" (Von Franz 207).

Her colleagues applaud her when she walks in and Thompson welcomes her. By saving New York, she's won multiple battles, and also made peace with the one inside – she's found her calling. However, when he's offered a senator's compliments, he doesn't share credit. While Daniel is appalled, Peggy replies, "I don't need a congressional honor. I don't need Agent Thompson's approval or the president's. I know my value. Anyone else's opinion doesn't really matter" ("Valediction," 1.8). To background music of "The Way You Look Tonight," a song about preserving a memory, she pours out Steve's blood and finds closure as she says goodbye at last. Inside, she's found completion.

VALERIE ESTELLE FRANKEL

Reconciling the Spilt Self: Daredevil

Daredevil, the first TV-MA series in the Marvel Cinematic Universe, arrived less than a month before *Avengers: Age of Ultron,* as the hype was building. Based on Frank Miller's "The Man Without Fear", the show is dark, gritty, and brutal. *Daredevil* is the first of many Netflix series: Next planned are *A.K.A. Jessica Jones* (2015). *Iron Fist* (2015), and *Luke Cage* (2016), all leading up to an eventual crossover in *The Defenders.* Marvel's Head of Television Jeph Loeb explains:

> I brought to the group this idea of doing the street-level heroes and *The Defenders* story. We went to Netflix and brought them this idea that we would do four 13-part stories that would be separate, individual stories, but in their own way, would feel like they're part of the same universe. Then, those four characters would join together and be in something called *The Defenders.* And *Daredevil* would kick it off. ... There had to be Iron Man, The Hulk, Captain America and Thor, before you could make *The Avengers.* For us, Daredevil, Jessica Jones, Luke Cage and Iron Fist had to exist before you could make *The Defenders.* But we also needed something that was organic. We couldn't just randomly pick four characters and put them on a team and hope that it all worked out. These are characters that have known each other in the comics, and who have had relationships, in the case of Jessica and Luke Cage. It gave us the opportunity to really look at that, and to find the best place to tell those stories. (Radish)

Stan Lee imagined Daredevil as a "Scarlet Swashbuckler" and expert gymnast back in 1964. He had circus performer qualities including skills as escape artist, and a multicolored costume. While Stan notes that he "loved the idea of a blind man being able to accomplish things no sighted man could" (Lee and Mair 167) and many disabled fans were enthusiastic, the character seemed another Spider-Man swooping through New York. His plots were simplistic, mostly driven by the goofy villains. This is not the character as he is best known today.

Modern Daredevil is derived from Frank Miller's transformation of the character in the eighties. This was a grim antihero always worried about crossing the line into murder and true villainy. Miller brought in Kingpin as Matt Murdock's chief nemesis and Elektra as femme fatale. He invented Stick, who trained Matt in sensory perception instead of having Matt instantly acquire a full set of powers. He also incorporated chain-smoking Daily Bugle reporter Ben Urich as the ordinary man willing to make a difference. The show brings in all of this (though Elektra only gets a quick allusion to the "Greek girl" Matt dated in college). Miller returned to *Daredevil* in '93 to write *The Man Without Fear,* a five-issue miniseries with artist John Romita Jr. that rebooted Matt Murdock's origin. The show's flashbacks follow much of this, from Matt's black ninja outfit to Kingpin, and Matt's father refusing to take a dive for the Fixer, even while insisting Matt turn his back on boxing and study. Miller's Daredevil is admittedly harsher than the show's character – he kills on occasion, starting with his father's executioners. Likewise, the father is drunk and abusive, leading Matt to study law seeking justice in an unfair world.

In the comics, the mystery radiation that splashes in young Matt's eyes awakens a power. On the show, Stick calls him "Gifted," the MCU's word for mutants or other natural superhumans. Either way, of course, Matt's powers come from childhood trauma that has woken an abnormal ability. After a near-death experience, "colors seem sharper, family and friends are more important, and time is more precious. The nearness of death makes life more real" (Vogler 164). This becomes literally true for Matt, extending the metaphor into superpowers.

Matt Murdock is not the only disabled hero, merely the most blatantly so. Tony Stark with his terminal shrapnel and Bruce Banner with his split personality are depicted as managing "conditions." These disabilities can be flipped into strengths, much as Matt does. This also has roots in myth. "It is not by accident that the one-eyed, the lame, those with withered limbs or other physical differences have, through time, been sought out as possessing a special knowing. Their injury or difference forces them early on into parts of the psyche normally reserved for the very, very old" (Estés 463).

It's significant that unlike Captain America, Iron Man, Hulk, Thor, and the others of the MCU, Daredevil has a secret identity. He is as split as his worlds, into defender and criminal, righteous crusader for good and punisher of evil. Metaphorically, even the show is the dark underbelly of the MCU. Hell's Kitchen is a darker, more crime-filled world than the bright heroism of the Avengers, battling in the sky with godlike strength. No one onscreen cheers for the superheroes, only exploits the damaged property for their own gain. Matt and his friends lack the budget of Stark Industries or S.H.I.E.L.D. and must thump on the router to make the internet work. Violence and despair abound. Innocents die.

In the Frank Miller comic, the city roars, "You can't escape me...you can't escape yourself." Daredevil (Charlie Cox) is the denizen of the dark city, and with her shocking push into murder and corporate crime, his new friend Karen Page (Deborah Ann Woll) finds herself there as well. She protests, "I don't see the city any more – all that I see are its dark corners." Matt's best friend Foggy attempts to reassure her, introducing her to the shady-looking characters at the bar, then reassuring her until daylight ("Cut Man," 1.2). "This city's beautiful," Foggy says after showing Karen its best aspects. Claire Temple, Matt's night nurse, also inspires him, though she demands answers to the tough moral questions. She is the first person with whom Matt shares his identity. Estés describes the process of healing from rage – seeking a wise mentor as healing force (Stick), accepting the challenge of exploring new psychic territory by questing into unfamiliar places (Matt begins saving others in costume), recognizing illusions, laying one's old patterns of thinking to rest, (much like Matt's father's boxing gear in its chest), healing the compassionate self (saving gentle Karen) and finally accepting the pain of the savage side of the self – becoming Daredevil (Estés 380). In all of this, Matt's allies are essential.

While Claire is his principles, Karen and Foggy both represent Matt's innocence, pushing him to hope for a better world and live the right way, even as Kingpin and the city itself drag him into despair. Their insistence on teamwork even in the bad times is a constant pillar of Matt's life. Elden Henson (Foggy) explains:

> That was one of the characteristics of Foggy that I latched onto was the real love for his friends and not just his friends but the people around him, his neighborhood. I identified with that because I have the same five friends that I've had ever since I can remember and we all still get together. I consider my friends my brothers and my brothers my best friends so that was really easy to fall into. (Halterman)

In Frank Miller's origin story, Matt has the corporate job and Foggy, battling a slumlord, is the one who inspires him to fight for the downtrodden of Hell's Kitchen. In both mediums, he's Matt's inspiration to keep fighting for goodness.

Another source of hope in the world is the church, especially for Matt. Religious iconography is heavy as Matt Murdock begins the series with confession. "I'm not seeking penance for what I've done, Father. I'm asking for forgiveness... for what I'm about to do" ("Into the Ring," 1.1). During his confession, Matt reveals much about his father the boxer and the fact his grandma claimed the Murdock boys "got the devil in 'em." Already he is being dragged into darkness as he struggles toward the light. His duty is framed as religious – Daredevil calls taking extraordinary beatings without complaint "Catholicism" (1.2). He was raised by nuns, at least for a time. Episode nine sees him discussing the concept of evil with his priest, especially whether it is an evil act to kill a villain and what the act will do to Matt. In episode three, Murdock's wounded side emphasizes his status as Christ figure. A church with angel statue shows up in the credits, right before the Daredevil mask, setting them in opposition. He is the protector of the significantly named "Hell's Kitchen," ordering several criminals out of "his" city. Despite his goodness, he strikes fear and suspicion into the people around him so that they equate him with his hellish origins. He soon becomes known as "the devil of Hell's Kitchen."

Frank Miller's comic arc *Born Again* emphasizes Matt's connection with the church as a mysterious nun counsels him when he's first blinded, then heals him in a time of total despair, in a plot reminiscent of Biblical Job. During his decent into hell and back, Daredevil clings to his religious faith, something rare in comic book superheroes.

By contrast, supervillain Wilson Fisk's first appearance comes in the closest the show offers to heaven – a light-filled, elegant gallery flooded with classical music. Fisk (Vincent D'Onofrio), in a suit, stands motionless, watching a white on white painting. It makes him feel "alone," much like God himself, towering over the world from his home in the sky. The painting, of, one might say, a rabbit in a snowstorm, emphasizes how he blends into this world. His next appearance sees him on an elegant date with the gallery owner Vanessa (Ayelet Zurer). Marvel's Head of Television Jeph Loeb explains:

> One of the other things – and it's something that Steven handled so well – is that part of what is so horrific about that Wilson Fisk scene doesn't have to do with the violence of it. To me, it's because you've spent an entire episode watching this man go on a date. You've been watching him be a gentleman, and really a gentle man. Ayelet Zurer's performance opposite Vincent D'Onofrio really lets them play off one another. Vincent's interpretation of the character is that he's playing a child who is also a monster. You're very much starting to root for Wilson, and you're starting to hope that this love story is going to be okay. Then, he does this terrible thing and you suddenly think, "Oh, that's why he's this horrible person we all know!" (Radish)

Elden Henson (Foggy) adds of the villain: "There's a real humanity there and it almost makes his character scarier in a way… It was apparent to me that all the characters on the show would have somewhere to go" (Halterman).

Hero and villain are shadows, emphasized in the fourth episode. Both glide through the world anonymously, speaking in whispering voices, known as the "employer" and the "man in black." Wilson Fisk is only named in the third episode, by a hired killer who immediately kills himself, filled with fear over the name he's revealed. "Do you know why Fisk doesn't want anyone saying his name," one of the Russian brothers says. "Because it would betray that he's just a man" ("In the Blood," 1.4).

"So's the guy in the mask and look what he's done to us," the other says.

In fact, Fisk wears all black, just like his counterpart. Matt feels guilt for causing his father's death, while Fisk killed his father more literally. They are both also sons of Hell's Kitchen. Fisk tells

Vanessa, "I realized that the city was a part of me, that it was in my blood. And I would do anything to make it a better place for people like you." Daredevil says something similar at episode end. They share the same goal but different methods, as Daredevil saves the helpless and Kingpin uses them. Both show how far they'll go for the women who attract them – Daredevil beats up Russian mobster Vladimir to save Claire Temple, while Kingpin beats up the Russian's brother Anatoli as an act of revenge because, as he says, "You embarrassed me ... embarrassed me in front of her."

In episode six, hero and villain finally speak, via police radio.

> Fisk: You and I have a lot in common
> Murdock: We're nothing alike.
> Fisk: That's what you'll tell yourself...I want to save this city, like you, only on a scale that matters.

Fisk tells him he understands the desire to rebuild the world with his own two hands "but we both can't have what we want." He frames Daredevil for his own crimes. "I respect your conviction, even if it runs counter to my own," Fisk adds.

In episode nine, they meet in person. Upon seeing lawyer Matt Murdock, Fisk launches into his speeches about urban renewal.

> Fisk: This city and its future...is very important to me.
> Matt: I feel the same way.

Once more they're linked. More, Matt learns "that he has someone who loves him...who would mourn his loss." Though he insists he hopes to discover Fisk is a monster, he instead finds they are much the same. The right thing to do grows clouded and uncertain. "Healing is in the process of questing and practice, not in a single idea" especially if that idea is execution (Estés 381). Watching him on television, Matt decides he's sincere about fixing the city. Later that episode, they meet as Kingpin the crime lord and Daredevil, and they battle. As a result, Daredevil is nearly killed and must reveal himself to Foggy – all his secrets are coming out thanks to the shadow's provocative presence.

Throughout the show, there's a strong emphasis on duality: there are only two sides – the good guys and the bad. "You don't carry a masked man bleeding to death into your apartment on faith. You knew which side you were on the moment you found me,"

Daredevil tells his new friend and savior Claire. In fact she reveals that she's heard of the masked man and all he does to save the innocents of her community. She even tells Daredevil how to torture a kidnapper. Charlie Cox explains, "There are so many aspects. There's the blindness and physicality. Making a show is about human emotion, conflict and turmoil. When meeting a man who's a lawyer by day and believes in law and justice and then a man by night is someone who takes the law into his own hands. He deals with battles dealing with that concept" (Brooks).

In his courtroom speech of episode three, defending Fisk's hired killer John Healey, Murdock explains: "I've been preoccupied of late with questions of morality, of right and wrong, good and evil. Sometimes the delineation between the two is a sharp line. Sometimes it's a blur. And often it's like pornography – you just know it when you see it." In his world, there are no shades of grey, only the sharp line between doing what is right and what is wrong. In the courtroom, as he tells the jury, they all, including him, must uphold the law. Still, as he ends his speech by emphasizing "beyond these walls, he may well face a judgment of his own making" the audience understands that Daredevil will takes steps Matt Murdock cannot.

Daredevil is very much Matt's shadow – all the things he won't let himself do in the daylight. As he threatens a thuggish kidnapper, he tells the darkest, most shameful secrets: "I need you to know why I'm hurting you. It's not just the boy. I'm doing this because I enjoy it" ("Cut Man," 1.2). He throws the villain off the roof in a particularly non-superheroic move.

Marvel's Head of Television Jeph Loeb explains: "There is no one who is more conflicted in the Marvel Universe, in my opinion, than Matthew Murdock. Is he his father's son, or is he the son of his father? Is he someone who is going to solve the world's problems in a courtroom, or is he someone who is going to solve the world's problems with his fist?" (Radish).

Matt appears to abandon everything Daredevil stands for as he protests his friends trying to stop Fisk. "I don't want anyone to be a hero, Karen. I want you to be safe. And I wanna protect this firm and everything we're trying to build here. We know the law, and we use it to our advantage" ("Shadows in the Glass," 1.8). He ends the series taking Fisk down with both sides of his personality – revealing his crimes to the world by persuading his client to offer evidence, then capturing Fisk in new Daredevil costume, battling the supervillain to a standstill and turning him over to the police. Matt has reconciled his two halves, uniting all his skills to end the terror. He no longer denies or separates from his shadow side but embraces it. "Allowing oneself to be taught by one's rage, thereby transforming it, disperses it. One's energy returns to use in other areas, especially the area of creativity" (Estés 382). His reimagined costume emphasizes his new statement of certainty.

"Generally speaking, a hero's costume (the sign of his superpowers) is linked in some (permanently visible) way with his origin" The costume is generally connected with the transformation: "Tony Stark's Iron Man costume began as an extension of the chest plate needed to aid his diseased heart. Spider-Man's costume portrays and externalizes Peter Packer's spider-like and spider-derived powers. Captain America's red, white, and blue appropriate and mobilize the patriotic emotions attendant on the character's creation" (Reynolds 49). Daredevil dresses as what others have named him – the devil of Hell's Kitchen, complete with horns, a blazing red mystery presence that echoes his perception of a world "on fire" as well as his religious conflict.

Although Daredevil's costume is most well known as red (from the Ben Affleck film as well as *Secret Wars*), the original comic book costume was yellow and brown. Frank Miller was the one to dress him in black in his own origin story. The red and black both offer clearer iconography. The black is simplistic and shadowed – the city's mystery ninja defender. By contrast, the red is a proud superheroic statement, like Matt's father going into the ring. It also speaks of sacrifice and martyrdom – "The good thing about red – you can't tell how much you're bleeding," Young Matt says of his father's last costume (1.2).

Equally crimson is the opening title sequence, created by Elastic, who previously created the thematically appropriate titles for *True Detective*. DeKnight explained that multiple companies had made pitches to the creative team involving "variations of the same idea, where you zoom in on an eye and you see a sonar map of the city." However, one of Elastic's pitches had "fluid-like blood dripping over everything ... as if paint were covering something invisible and revealing it," which both DeKnight and Loeb wanted to use immediately (Radish). It echoes Daredevil's means of perception, fuzzy, as if everything is on fire, as he tells Claire in episode five. Obviously it also nods to the blood and violence of Daredevil's life, outlining the city he struggles to protect.

Easter Eggs

Iron Man

- Stane tells Tony, "That's what we do. We're iron mongers. We make weapons." In the comics, the Ironmonger is his superhero name.
- Coulson shows up and discusses S.H.I.E.L.D., finally shortening it to its acronym.
- Captain America's iconic shield can be seen in the background of Tony's lab being worked on.
- When Tony calls Rhodey, his ringtone is the theme to the 1966 "Iron Man" cartoon. The theme music also pops up as part of Stark's wake-up sequence in his bedroom, at the Apogee Award ceremony and in the casino.
- The leader of the terrorist kidnappers is called Raza. This may nod to the existing Marvel character Raza – an alien cyborg member of the Starjammers, a group of space pirates.
- The stewardesses on the plane dance to "We Celebrate" by Ghostface Killah – a hip-hop artist who sometimes uses the aliases "Ironman" and "Tony Starks."
- At the end of the film, Stark reads a newspaper with a fuzzy, amateur image of Iron Man. This is actually a fan's capture of filming leaked online prior to the film's release.
- The terrorist organization that kidnaps Tony call themselves "The Ten Rings," a nod to the Mandarin's comics organization.

- While chasing Iron Man, one of the jet fighter's call names is Whiplash, a comics villain who appears in *Iron Man 2*

- Rhodey eyes the spare Iron Man suit and says, "next time baby." In fact, the actor's replacement, Don Cheadle wears it in the sequels.

- During the climactic battle with Iron Monger the building in the background bears a Roxxon Corporation logo. They are a frequent *Iron Man* antagonist.

- A Fin Fang Foom poster appears. He is a dragon-like alien created for Marvel by Stan Lee.

- Obadiah Stane is shown playing a game of chess. In the comics, Stane formed a team to attack Iron Man called the Chessmen.

- Christine Everhart, the blonde journalist following Tony throughout the first two *Iron Man* films is a preexisting Marvel character, who usually works for the *Daily Bugle* rather than *Vanity Fair*.

- Stan Lee Cameo: Tony Stark mistakes him for Hugh Hefner.

- Post-credits: Nick Fury shows up to discuss the Avengers.

The Incredible Hulk

Thunder clap, we wanted to do it. The Hulk speaking, we wanted to do it. The purple pants, I wanted to address because I thought it was fun. But like Dr. Reinstein and Vita Rays, that actually was done on the day because we wanted the super serum. And the prop master said, "What do you want me to do with this?" And I said, "OK. Give me the serum." And he said, "What color should the serum be?" I said, "Blue like Captain America and I want the cap for the vial to be red like Captain America." And he said, "What do you want me to put on the sticker?" And I gave him Dr. Reinstein and Vita Rays; you know... the nerdy stuff. And there's tons more; the more you see the movie, you'll see tons and tons of stuff. This is my first Marvel movie. This is my first attempt at a superhero that has a history that's loved all around so I wanted to pay homage to both the TV show... You'll see. There's Johnson Base, which is from [TV show creator] Kenneth Johnson, Bill Bixby on the TV screen... tips of the hat to all of these people. This is the stuff that to me was important to do because... some of the stuff I'm a fan of. (Leterrier)

- The equipment of the intro closely resembles that seen in the TV series.

- In a deleted/alternate opening to *The Incredible Hulk* we see the Capsicle himself (with shield) frozen in ice.

- The name Sterns uses during his correspondence with Banner – Mr. Blue – comes from Bruce Jones' run on Hulk, where Betty Ross used this alias to communicate with Hulk while he was on the run.

- In a deleted scene, Blonsky describes his first encounter with the Hulk and says "8 foot, 1500 pounds easy... and green. Or grey, sir. Greenish-grey. It was very dark, I couldn't tell." This references the Hulk's colouring problems in early versions of the comic, in which grey soon became green.

- "You wouldn't like me when I'm hungry" is an obvious pun.

- The opening S.H.I.E.L.D. files mention Rick Jones, Hulk's human confidante and later a superhero in his own right.

- In *The Ultimates,* as with this film, Bruce's Hulking resulted from an attempt to recreate the Captain America serum.

- Stanley's Pizza is a pun on Stan Lee. Also, the owner of the pizza shop is the same actor who voiced Bruce Banner in the 1966 Hulk cartoon.

- Lou Ferrigno, the iconic star of the original 70s show, cameos as Security Guard. He also voices the Hulk in this film and in *The Avengers.*

- Fan favorite comics character Doc Samson is Betty Ross's new man, albeit without his trademark long green hair.

- The composer uses the Bill Bixby TV show theme, especially when Bruce hitchhikes down the road.
- The redacted S.H.I.E.L.D. files imply that the Hulk film from 2003 fits into canon. These have Nick Fury's name printed on them and also mention of Rick Jones; the man Banner sacrificed himself to save from gamma radiation in the comics.
- General Ross dusts off a Stark Industries brand serum to give Blonsky, labeled with the name Dr. Reinstein from *Captain America.*
- Weapons PLUS references the Weapon's program that created Wolverine and Deadpool.
- When Betty Ross goes shopping for Bruce she returns with extremely large, very familiar, purple pants.
- Culver University references the Culver Institute, where Banner first exposed himself to Gamma radiation in the TV series.
- Student eyewitnesses to the fight between the Hulk and General Ross include Jack McGee and Jim Wilson. Jack McGee was the journalist who chased Banner through over half the episodes of the 70s TV show, and Jim Wilson was the nephew of the Falcon, a friend and sidekick of the Hulk.
- In *The Ultimates* comic, Fury orders the Hulk hurled from a plane to transform him into his counterpart.
- Banner receives a package addressed to his alias, "David B.," nodding to the fact that Banner would give himself a different surname beginning with B in each episode of the TV series.
- The late Bill Bixby from the show appears thanks to a scene from the movie *The Courtship of Eddie's Father,* playing on a TV screen in the background,
- Dr. Samuel Sterns (Tim Blake Nelson) ends up with the Hulk's radioactive blood dripping into an open head wound and his entire head begins to expand. The Leader, Hulk's nefarious nemesis, has been born, all prepared for the Hulk sequel that was tabled afterward.

- While fighting Blonsky, the Hulk tears a police car in half and uses the pieces like boxing gloves. This ability was first seen in the popular video game, *The Incredible Hulk: Ultimate Destruction* (2005).
- Stan Lee drinks the Hulk-blood soda.
- Post-credits Tony Stark approaches General Ross and brings up the Avengers Initiative. More backstory appears in the first ever Marvel One-Shot. "The Consultant" (available on the *Thor* Blu-Ray), which shows Coulson and Sitwell trying to keep Emil Blonsky out of The Avengers Initiative, so they send in the irritating Tony Stark to invite him.

Captain America

- When Bucky and Steve Rogers enter Stark Expo, the bright red jumpsuit on display is from the original Human Torch, Marvel's very first character, back when it was called Timely Comics. (Ironically Chris Evans, Captain America, played the other Marvel Human Torch in the *Fantastic Four* movies owned by Fox.)
- At the Expo, Howard Stark has a problematic hovercar, a precursor to Lola as well as Tony's repulsors. Of course, all his appearances in the film tie this to the *Iron Man* series, as well as (much later) *Agent Carter*.
- The Norse mythological world tree Yggdrasill is seen here in an ancient chamber behind Red Skull. Thor draws this in his film to show Jane Foster the concept of the Nine Realms.
- During his war bonds skit Cap punches an actor dressed as Hitler in the face, nodding to the iconic cover for "Captain America #1."
- Soldier Gilmore Hodge is from the comics.
- The first shot of Arnim Zola is through a huge magnifying glass, giving him the giant head on a screen look he has in the comics. The schematics of this very look are on the table next to him. Zola grabs plans for

his comics robot suit as he escapes. Later, in *Winter Soldier,* we actually see Zola as face on screen.

- Right before "dying," Bucky wields Cap's shield in much the same pose he would later in the comics when he goes from being *The Winter Soldier* to taking on the Captain America mantle outright.

- Captain America's World War 2 team, the Howling Commandos, combines his comic book team the Howling Commandos and the Invaders, a group of superheroes that Captain America led in the 1970s (including Bucky and James Montgomery Falsworth).

- Whedon, director of *The Avengers,* did a script treatment for this film.

- Stan Lee Cameo: He's a general in World War II, who mistakes a random man for Captain America.

Iron Man 2

- The superheroes hotspots map includes the locations of Wakanda (Black Panther) in Africa, and Prince Namor in the Atlantic.

- The same scene features a news report from Culver University – spotted by Hulk movie fans, no doubt, as the location for Big Green's battle with General Ross's men

- As Tony looks through his father's belongings he lifts some papers and briefly reveals a corner of an old *Captain America* comic book cover.

- A hypercube is seen in Howard Stark's notes.

- During the opening talks with Senator Stern, Tony says he wouldn't mind being given the Secretary of Defense position... This actually did happen in the comics 2004 storyline, *The Best Defense.*

- Howard Stark's presentation of "The city of tomorrow" is closely modeled on Walt Disney's presentation of Epcot, the "Experimental Prototype Community of Tomorrow" before it was turned into a theme park. The Stark Expo layout is based on the 1964

New York World's Fair. The building Stark picks up is the Bell System Pavilion.

- At one point, Stark calls the government the "Freak Brothers." *The Fabulous Furry Freak Brothers* is one of the seminal works of the underground comix.
- Natasha changes in the backseat and orders Happy Hogan to stop staring at her. This was a staple of her comics.
- A half-constructed Captain America shield can be seen when Agent Coulson hands him it to balance out the equipment he uses to create a new element.
- Fury mentions the Southwest where the hammer fell, and Coulson mentions New Mexico
- Circuits Maximus is from the comics
- Stan Lee Cameo: Tony Stark mistakes him for Larry King while leaving a gala.
- Post-credits: Mjolnir has crashed to earth

Thor

- Odin's treasure room has several comic book artifacts: the orb of agamato, the Tablet of Life and Time, the Eternal Flame, the Warlock's Eye and the all-important Infinity Gauntlet, which holds the Infinity Stones of the larger MCU Arc.
- The Tesseract is seen briefly in Erik Selvig's book on Norse mythology with an illustration of Odin carrying the cube.
- Odin's two ravens appear.
- The town's name means old bridge – and it's where the rainbow bridge ends
- In the original run of *Thor*, the mighty god was sent down to earth and into the body of disabled med-student, Donald Blake. This is Thor's fake ID from New York in the film.
- During the banquet, writer Walt Simonson is seated directly next to Sif.

- A billboard is seen advertising New Mexico as the "Land of Enchantment... Journey into Mystery." The character of Thor debuted in the *Journey into Mystery* comic series before getting his own.

- Dr Selvig mentions that he knew a colleague who encountered S.H.I.E.L.D. and describes him as "a pioneer in gamma radiation" – a clear reference to Bruce Banner.

- Stan Lee Cameo: Stan Lee is in the truck trying to pull Mjolnir out of the ground. Writer J. Michael Straczynski also tries to lift the hammer

- Post credits: Nick Fury shows the Tesseract to Selvig, who asks what it is, to which Fury replies "unlimited power." Whedon, director of *The Avengers*, directed this scene.

The Avengers

- Ironically, Whedon had no desire to work with the Avengers originally. In 2005, he said, "Y'know, the thing about the *X-Men* is they have a coherent core. *The Avengers* to me is tough. I wouldn't approach *The Avengers*, I wouldn't approach the *Fantastic Four*. The *X-Men* are all born of pain, and pain is where I hang my hat" (Kozak). Clark Gregg (Agent Coulson) notes:

> To whatever extent this was the plan, Marvel has done these origin movies—which you know, if they didn't work there never would have been an Avengers. I think if even one of them had been a big bomb, I don't think they ever would have given them the money to make The Avengers. But they pulled it off and they got all these people invested in these characters and feeling kind of like new fanboys and fangirls, who are now going the other way and starting to buy some comics." (Burlingame)

- The movie obviously combines characters and events from the other movies: *Iron Man, Iron Man 2, Thor, Captain America,* and *The Incredible Hulk.* Only the Hulk was recast.

- The line "Avengers Assemble" is only used sarcastically by Stark, but is the movie title in the UK.

- Captain America, Hawkeye, and Black Widow dress like their *Ultimate* incarnations, but act more like their main universe counterparts.

- Thor's costume takes elements from his original costume, the *Ultimate* line, and his contemporary comic outfit.

- Banner wears a purple shirt for most of the film, subtly nodding to Hulk's iconic purple pants.

- The early battle explores hierarchical continuity in a nod to fans—based on which villains they've defeated, who is actually stronger, Cap or Iron Man? What if the Hulk's Hammer (all powerful) hits Cap's shield (all-defensible)?

- In the comics, both Hawkeye and Black Widow started out as villains (they were even partnered together!) before reforming. In The Avengers film, Hawkeye becomes evil (temporarily) and Black Widow mentions her dark past.

- Nick Fury is played by Samuel L. Jackson. His original character was white, but the *Ultimate* Universe drew him as Jackson, setting him up for this role far in advance.

- The Avengers movie gets in some name references and catchphrases:

Captain America says: "And Hulk...Smash."
Hulk calls Loki a "puny god," referencing his catchphrase in the comics, "puny human!"
"If we can't protect the Earth, you can be damned well sure we'll avenge it," Stark says.
"It's alright, sir. This was never going to work unless they had something...to..." "avenge" probably ends Coulson's dying line.

- While talking to Loki, Tony calls the Avengers "Earth's mightiest heroes," and says "Avengers, Assemble."

- The Avengers takes its storyline from the first issues of *Avengers* (1963-64) with Loki setting Thor against the Hulk. His scheme backfires and the Avengers unite. Also, in *The Ultimates,* Nick Fury, head of S.H.I.E.L.D., leads the Avengers against the invading Chitauri.

- In the movies, the Tesseract is a powerful item that the Red Skull found (in Captain America) and Loki steals (in Avengers). The comics have the Cosmic Cube, a reality-warping device that Hydra covets.

- Selvig reports "Nothing harmful, low levels of gamma radiation." Fury retorts, "That can be harmful. This was what transformed the Hulk."

- Georgi Luchkow, the Russian Black Widow beats up early on, is a minor Black Widow villain from the early '90s.

- "You have reached the Life Model Decoy of Tony Stark," Tony mouths off. Life Model Decoy is the comic book term for robotic clones of characters.

- Banner mentions that at one point, he tried to kill himself with a pistol "and the other guy spat out the bullet." This was planned as the opening of The Incredible Hulk film (and appeared in the Alt-Universe miniseries "Banner!")

- The Captain America trading cards display artwork by Jack Kirby.

- The Tesseract facility at the movie's start is called Project Pegasus, a S.H.I.E.L.D. research site from the comics.

- Thor's lightning supercharges Iron Man's armor in their first battle in the comics and in the movie.

- Hulk chases Black Widow similarly to the Iron Man movie scene in which Iron Monger chases Pepper Potts.

- Hulk died in the TV show by falling out of an aircraft and landing as Banner. The air-drop prison is a reference.

- "The staircase" where Loki meets the Chitauri leader "The Other" is a creative reference to the work of seminal Avengers writer and artist Jim Starlin.
- The movie rights to Skrulls are tied up with the Fantastic Four, so The Avengers uses the Ultimate equivalent.
- Cap and Iron Man's tag-team move is from *Marvel Ultimate Alliance 2.*
- The character Shawna Lynde is from 1980s Thor comics.
- The *World War Hulk* arc is built around the concept that he's always angry and thus can easily shift.
- The Hulk leaps out at a Chitauri ship much like the way Mr. Incredible attacked the Omnidroid 10.0.
- At the end, Senator Boynton asks where the Avengers are. He's a minor figure from the *Armor Wars* storyline.
- Stark Tower's "STARK" logo is battered, leaving a stylish "A," like the classic "Avengers" logo.
- Project Pegasus becomes a superhero prison.
- Stan Lee Cameo: He ended up playing a man interviewed for TV who doesn't believe that the Avengers are real, saying "Superheroes? In New York? Give me a break!" There's also a deleted scene with a brief interaction between Lee and Steve Rogers.
- Post credits: Thanos and the Other scheme, preparing for *Guardians of the Galaxy.* In the comic books, Thanos falls in love with Death after he sees her. Notably, he smiles on the show when saying "To challenge them is to court death."

Iron Man 3

- In *Iron Man 3*'s opening flashback, Tony Stark is seen briefly being introduced to Dr Yinsen at a conference in Switzerland, as the scientist mentions in the first film.
- Aldrich Killian's company in *Iron Man 3* is Advanced Idea Mechanics, a huge criminal organization in the comics that is sometimes aligned with Hydra.

- The president is named Ellis, a nod to noted *Iron Man* writer Warren Ellis.

- When the Mandarin removes his hood, a tattoo of Cap's Shield with an "A" for "anarchy" is revealed: he's clearly anti-establishment.

- Ten rings appear as the Mandarin's slogan.

- When Stark signs an autograph for two kids, he tells one of them that he looks like Ralphie Packer from *A Christmas Story*. The actor who played Ralphie, Peter Billingsley, was a producer on the first two *Iron Man* films.

- The kid suggests stealth mode, which comics Tony makes.

- Ellen Brant and Taggert are both from the comics.

- The scenes outside Killian's AIM headquarters were filmed at Epic Games in North Carolina, a creator of the Unreal engine, enabling games of many franchises.

- The climactic scene takes place on a Roxxon tanker.

- When the explosive villain kneels down at Grauman's, Downey's actual handprints can be seen in the cement.

- Happy Hogan addresses an off-camera Stark Enterprises secretary as "Bambi" – this is Bambi Arbogast, Stark's long-time secretary in the comics.

- Stan Lee Cameo: He rates girls in the beauty contest.

- Post-Credits: Stark has been telling the entire story to Bruce Banner, who fell asleep at the beginning of it.

Marvel One-Shots

- "The Consultant" (2011) After Iron Man 2 and The Incredible Hulk, the World Security Council wishes Emil Blonsky released from prison to join the Avengers Initiative. However, Fury is horrified, so he has Phil Coulson and Jasper Sitwell arrange for Tony Stark to approach General Thaddeus "Thunderbolt" Ross. Coulson sends "The Consultant": Tony Stark, and the deal goes flat. This scene emphasizes how S.H.I.E.L.D. is pulling the strings behind many events.

- "A Funny Thing Happened on the Way to Thor's Hammer" (2011): Stopping at a gas station, Coulson is held up but takes down the robbers, showing that he's more than a bureaucrat.

- "Item 47" (2012) Lizzy Caplan and Jesse Bradford play an unlucky couple who find a discarded Chitauri gun after The Avengers and use it to rob banks. Agents Sitwell and Blake chase them down and invite them to join S.H.I.E.L.D. Sitwell and Blake appeared in Agents of S.H.I.E.L.D. and Winter Soldier.

- "Agent Carter" (2013) stars Hayley Atwell as Peggy Carter after Captain America, but before her own show. While working for SSR, Peggy gets a call from Howard Stark, telling her she is to co-head the newly created S.H.I.E.L.D. Dum Dum Dugan cameos, admiring bikinis beside Stark. Captain America archive footage appears as well.

- "All Hail the King" (2014) stars Ben Kingsley as Trevor Slattery after the events of Iron Man 3. Held in Seagate Prison, he meets Justin Hammer from Iron Man 2, and discusses his life with a documentary filmmaker, Jackson Norriss. Norriss eventually informs Slattery that the actual Ten Rings terrorist group and Mandarin are furious with him, though Slattery remains relatively naïve about his predicament.

Agents of S.H.I.E.L.D.

- Characters on *Agents of S.H.I.E.L.D.* often discuss Black Widow and Hawkeye. Nick Fury and Maria Hill visit for multiple episodes, as does Sif.

- Both Skye (episode one) and Steve Rogers say they'll never see anything new again, and then get a shock.at the new tech.

- Coulson gives the new, uncertain team a common enemy in "0-8-4" (AS1.2) and *The Avengers*.

- Skye tells Mike that "with great power comes...a ton of weird crap that you're not ready for!" a riff on the line from *Spider-Man* (Pilot).

- At the end of the pilot, Coulson quips that they must "cut the head off the Centipede," echoing Hydra's motto, "Cut off one head, two more will take its place."

- The website *The Rising Tide* shows clips from the Marvel movies resembling poorly filmed camcorder footage.

- Characters are described as "Gifted," because the show doesn't have the rights to *X-Men*'s mutants.

- Ward is recovering from a "Chitauri neural link" after *The Avengers*. He's described as having the highest grades as a Stealth Expert since Romanov.

- Coulson's "Welcome to Level 7" answers Jasper Sitwell's question in "The Consultant" ("Come on, there's a level 7?").

- Coulson's mobile command is designated S.H.I.E.L.D. 616, after the primary Marvel comics universe, Universe 616. The official name for the Bus – Mobile Command Unit, or MCU, nods to Marvel Cinematic Universe. The "616 universe" refers to the multiversal designation number of the main Marvel Universe as assigned by the Omniversal Majestrix of Otherworld.

- Maria Hill is in the first episode, and Fury's in the second.

- The Centipede project looks to combine the Extremis virus (*Iron Man 3*) with gamma radiation (which created the Hulk) and Dr. Erskine's superserum (which created Captain America) to create new supersoldiers. The first user of the Centipede device mimics *The Incredible Hulk* movie, yelling at the lab worker, "I want to feel more!" Mike notes that the change depends on "what kind of person you are," a nod to the *Captain America* movie.

- Howard Stark invented an anti-grav car in the 1940s, like Lola. In the S.H.I.E.L.D. comics, flying cars supplied by Stark Industries have been standard since 1967.

- The 0-8-4 is Hydra tech. Reyes also mentions the fall of Hydra and their Nazi allies ("0-8-4," AS1.2).
- Skye mentions that S.H.I.E.L.D. had covered up New Mexico's Thor visit and Project Pegasus (where they were studying the Tesseract).
- Simmons asks Skye if she is ready to join them on their "journey into mystery," a Marvel Comics anthology title.
- "Technically Stark's a consultant" ("0-8-4," AS1.2) is an *Iron Man* nod. Agent Coulson starred in a video short about his dealings with Stark called "The Consultant."
- The last dangerous artifact that S.H.I.E.L.D. designated an "0-8-4," was apparently Thor's hammer Mjolnir, which appeared on Earth before Thor himself in another Marvel short movie featuring Coulson, "A Funny Thing Happened on the Way to Thor's Hammer."
- Coulson mentions cleaning up a fragment of Anti-Matter that crashed down near Miami – the Anti-Matter Universe comes from the *Fantastic Four* ("0-8-4," AS1.2). Fitz-Simmons say, "Take that, Professor Vaughn!"
- The Holographic Interface is from the *Iron Man* films.
- Supervillain Graviton was created in the Rockies, according to the comics. On Agents of S.H.I.E.L.D., his origin story episode has a truck marked "Rocky Mountain Office Supplies" ("The Asset," AS1.3).
- Coulson mentions sacrificing his card collection to help Fury in "The Asset" (AS1.3). Agent Tyler reappears.
- Echoing "Eye Spy" (AS1.4) there are many Marvel characters with cybernetic eyes, including Cable, Revanche and Crossfire.
- The equation that Ward photographs in "Eye-Spy" (AS1.4) has some sections written in Skrull. Later, Garrett and Coulson are seen writing it.

- Skye says "bang" when she pulls a trigger, an amusing nod to the comic book text bubbles.

- Akela mentions that she was held prisoner in the small village of Shang-Chi. This is a criminal mastermind in the Marvel universe.

- In "The Girl in the Flower Dress" (AS1.5), Coulson blows the lock with the same device he used in *Iron Man* to enter Obadiah Stane's workshop with Pepper Potts.

- Some are claiming that Scorch might be a version of Tommy Ng, a half-Vietnamese villain who fought Night Thrasher under the alias Scorch, but this Chinese character named Chan Ho Yin doesn't seem to fit.

- It's suggested that Scorch gained his pyrokinetic abilities thanks to a nuclear plant that caught fire near his house. Coulson fears his getting a superhero name will make him a monster. Both are common tropes.

- S.H.I.E.L.D's Index and Power Protocols echo the comic books' Superhero Registration Act, which plunged their world into civil war.

- The Bus's interrogation room is lined with a vibranium alloy, also used to create Captain America's shield.

- Skye makes an awkward *Big Lebowski* reference ("F.Z.Z.T.," AS1.6). Its star, Jeff Bridges, is Obadiah Stane in *Iron Man*.

- In "F.Z.Z.T.", Coulson and the gang are meant to be taking recovered Chitauri weapons to "the Sandbox," S.H.I.E.L.D.'s Moroccan office, There's no Sandbox in the comics, but Morocco is near Wakanda, home of Black Panther.

- "Item 47," a short on the *Avengers* Blue-Ray, featured criminals recruited to S.H.I.E.L.D. just as Skye was. In "F.Z.Z.T" (AS1.6), Agent Blake from this short appears.

- Agent Blake tells Coulson, "Someone might decide to take this dream team away from you." In fact, portions of S.H.I.E.L.D. go bad by *Captain America: The Winter Soldier.*

- Skye says Coulson is acting like "a robot version of himself" on "The Hub" (AS1.7). This appears to be red herring that Coulson is a life model decoy android.

- When the team walks through the Hub, there are numerous signs pointing to other divisions, such as H.A.M.M.E.R. or Sci Ops, A.R.M.O.R., and EuroMIND. These are straight from the Marvel Universe.

- Simmons notes that there's a S.H.I.E.L.D. base called the Triskelion that is even bigger than the Hub. Triskelion (on Governor's Island near Manhattan) comes from the *Ultimate* Marvel universe, and is also mentioned as a look-ahead to *Captain America: The Winter Soldier.*

- In the comics there are also eight levels of agents – Director Fury is the only occupant of Level Eight.

- Fury's old war buddies the Howling Commandos are mentioned. They appear in the *Captain America* movie.

- Agent Jasper Sitwell (played by Maximiliano Hernandez) is a longtime S.H.I.E.L.D. agent and frequent ally of Nick Fury in the comics. He appears in "The Hub" (AS1.7) as well as "Item 47," the Marvel One-Shot short film, with cameos in *Thor* and *Captain America: The Winter Soldier.*

- S.H.I.E.L.D. was infiltrated with shape-shifting aliens called Skrulls in the comics. (In the *Ultimate* universe, and in the movie, the name gets changed to the Chitauri.)

- Victoria Hand works for H.A.M.M.E.R. and S.H.I.E.L.D. in the comics, complete with the red streak in her hair.

- S.H.I.E.L.D.'s arch-nemesis agency, Hydra, builds the Overkill Horn in the comics, a sonic vibration doomsday device echoing the Overkill Device.

- Agents Barton and Romanov (Hawkeye and Black Widow) are mentioned in "The Hub" (AS1.7) as the only agents who don't use an extraction team.

- Watching Simmons jump out of the back of the S.H.I.E.L.D. bus, to be caught by Ward in mid-air echoes Iron Man's similar stunt in his third movie.

- "The Well" (AS1.8) picks up directly after the events of *Thor: The Dark World*, with the team cleaning up the city. As the so-called *Thor* tie-in, it's rather flimsy, with a movie montage, Asgardian protest group, superweapon, and warrior who decided to hang around on Earth.

- Berserkers in the Marvel Universe include a Morlock from under New York's subway system with electrokinetic powers, and a group given powers by Loki.

- Coulson's suggestion that Randolph move to Portland in "The Well" (AS1.8) is a callback to *The Avengers*. In episode ten, he mentions his lost girlfriend there, and she's seen near season's end.

- In "The Well" (AS1.8), Skye wonders whether gods from other pantheons, such as the Hindu deity Vishnu, exist as aliens. Vishnu made his first appearance in *Thor* #300.

- The gas station in the beginning of "Repairs" (AS1.9) is called "Roxxon," an Exxon parallel in the Marvel Comics.

- The Scrabble board shows the words strange and tales. *Strange Tales* is the comic book where Nick Fury debuted.

- In "Repairs" (AS1.9), the ship's visitor says he's trapped between our world and hell. This may be Surtur's realm.

- In "The Magical Place" (AS1.11), Fitz tells Simmons to "embrace the change." This was the catchphrase was the teaser for Marvel's 2008 multimedia event, *Secret Invasion*, in which Skrulls secretly replaced key people around the world. Is he an alien? It's unlikely, as after discovering Ward's defection, Fitz insists several times that he hates change. Chituri tech appears in the episode as well.

- Memory altering and amnesia happens to most Marvel heroes. Coulson spends the first season as one of them.

- In "The Magical Place" (AS1.11), Po is incapacitated by what appears to be the same sonic device used by Obadiah Stane in *Iron Man*. Raina claims Centipede and the Clairvoyant want to bring agents back from the dead. Baron Strucker of Hydra and *X-Men* enemy Mr. Sinister have mastered this in the comics.

- "Seeds" (AS1.12) references Vaughn and A.I.M. Quasar may be coming. The team visit S.H.I.E.L.D.'s academy, and Skye mentions Bucky Barnes, who's on the Wall of Valor.

- In "Seeds" (AS1.12) Supervillain Donnie Gill (Blizzard) – the *Iron Man* enemy and one-time Thunderbolts member – is introduced with a new backstory.

- "T.R.A.C.K.S." (AS1.13) offers the obligatory Stan Lee cameo on the train. Mike uses "Deathlok" technology, affirming his new identity. Coulson threatens to send Ward to Emil Blonsky and his "cryo-cell in Alaska," from *The Incredible Hulk*. Coulson adds he "can't deal with Asgard today."

- Agent John Garrett is a character from the *Elektra Assassin* run of Marvel comics.

- "T.A.H.I.T.I." (AS1.14) forces Coulson to confront his own mortality with Skye dying, echoing Nick Fury in *The Avengers* when Coulson is stabbed. May's beating Quinn in the interrogation room echoes Wolverine beating Crossbones after the assassination of *Captain America*.

- It's possible Agent Triplett is Triathalon, a gold medal sprinter who finds enlightenment with the Triune Understanding. Or he may be an original agent.

- The GH-325 source, a dissected blue alien floating in a tank, is a Kree, nodding to *Guardians of the Galaxy* and *The Inhumans*.

- Following the events of *Thor: The Dark World*, "Yes Men" (AS1.15) begins in a rural town like the first Thor. Lorelei and Sif explore the oh-so-different human world much as Thor does. Like Thor, Sif calls Coulson "Son of Coul." Lorelai escapes her captivity during *Thor: The Dark World*. Sif mentions the Kree and the Alpha Centaurians (along with Interdites, Levians, Pharagots and Sarks), in a shout out to *Guardians of the Galaxy*. Sif is serving Odin – problematic after *Thor: The Dark World*. She also compares May's relationship with Ward to her own with Thor.

- "The End of the Beginning" (AS1.16) offers a meeting with S.H.I.E.L.D. heads including Victoria Hand, Coulson, Jasper Sitwell, and Agent Blake. The phrase "Turn Turn Turn," the next week's episode, appears. It's suggested Hand is the Clairvoyant. (In the comics, she defects against S.H.I.E.L.D. for the more proactive and morally gray S.W.O.R.D. and H.A.M.M.E.R.) There's a shout out to Department H. The Fridge, the Marvel supervillain prison, is first mentioned here, and is visited in subsequent episodes.

- Mike Peterson looks exactly like the comic Deathlok on the x-ray screen, much to fans' delight.

- The dead partner, Dan Monroe, may be related to Captain America's partner Jack Monroe.

- The post credits tag of "End of the Beginning" (AS1.16) teases *Captain America: The Winter Soldier*. Sitwell's got a boat to catch (the "Lemurian Star" for the Lemurians, a type of mermaid), which he is on at the film's start.

- During "End of The Beginning," Agent Blake asks Melinda May if she's a Scorpio. Many spies for S.H.I.E.L.D. have had this name. May is revealed as a spy soon after.

- "Turn Turn Turn" (AS1.17), with constant references and some footage, is a complimentary production to *Captain America: The Winter Soldier*. Both sets of Fury's loyal agents battle Hydra as it takes over S.H.I.E.L.D. Garrett references Jasper Sitwell from the film. Fitz mentions he never distributed his "mouse hole" laser cutter, which Fury and Hill use in the movie. (Garrett mentions, "the top agents always want the good stuff for themselves.")

- "I wouldn't say I'm a true believer," Garrett tells Coulson in "Turn Turn Turn" (AS1.17). That's a nod to one of Stan Lee's famous *Mighty Marvel* catchphrases. The debate over cutting off a limb or a head contrasts Hydra's old and new mottos.

- In "Providence" (AS1.18), Coulson and Skye watch a report that replays *Captain America: The Winter Soldier.*

- Skye says they're "agents of nothing." *Nick Fury: Agent of Nothing,* a one-shot, set up *Secret Warriors,* a story about an unofficial team after S.H.I.E.L.D. gets disbanded.

- Ward brings Raina to meet Garrett in a barber shop in "Providence" (AS1.18). The barber chair that lowers into a secret S.H.I.E.L.D. base in New York is a comics staple.

- Eric Koenig, supervisor of Providence, first appeared in *Sgt Fury and his Howling Commandos* #27 (1966). A former member of Nazi Luftwaffehe became disenchanted with Hitler's ideology after the attack on Poland and recently died battling Hydra in the pages of *Secret Warriors.* While Patton Oswalt's Koenig is different, more like *Dollhouse*'s geeky software developer Joel Mynor (played by the same actor), they both are killed by Hydra

- Major Glenn Talbot, the U.S. government representative, annoyed the Hulk for years. General "Thunderbolt" Ross's right hand man, he was once married to Betty Ross, Bruce Banner's future wife.

- Coulson mentions the Cube is still functioning. It has a long history in S.H.I.E.L.D. lore.

- Hydra Agent Kaminsky is mentioned in "Providence" (AS1.18). This may actually be Arnold Kaminsky, owned by the *Fantastic Four* franchise. Johnny Horton, the villain known as the Griffin, is the villain who grafted lion paws onto his hands himself.

- In "The Only Light in the Darkness" (AS1.19), Patton Oswalt's Agent Koenig offers a lie detector that "even Romanov couldn't beat." Koenig asks each agent if they were connected to Alexander Pierce or Project Insight.

- Agent Koenig wishes he was descended from a Howling Commando…in the comics, he is one. Triplett's grandfather was apparently a Howling Commando – fans speculate it was Gabe Jones (played by Derek Luke and the only black Howling Commando in *Captain America: The First Avenger*). Meanwhile, Skye calls Eric Koenig "Steve Rogers," trying to get him to be braver ("The Only Light in the Darkness," AS1.19).

- Blackout, who first appeared in *Nova* #19 (May 1978), is the villain of "The Only Light in the Darkness" (AS1.19), similar to his comic book counterpart. The team use a gamma ray light weapon designed by Bruce Banner to bring him down. Blackout can use Darkforce, another Marvel staple. In the comics, Blackout can slip into the Darkforce Dimension, suggesting his explosion at episode end is not permanent.

- In "The Only Light in the Darkness" (AS1.19), Melinda Mae reveals her middle name is Qiaolian (her previous marriage comes up and viewers meet her mother as well). In *Iron Man: Titanium* #1, AIM villain Huang Qiaolian was introduced. (This is Advanced Idea Mechanics, the research division of Hydra that appears in *Iron Man 3*). Is May's mother connected to AIM?

- Maria Hill returns in "Nothing Personal" (AS 1.20). She talks to Pepper Potts on her cell and says she's going to work for Stark, quoting his *Iron Man 2* line of "privatizing world peace." Black Widow is mentioned, as are Coulson's and Nick Fury's "deaths."

- Maria Hill tells Pepper that Congress wanted to know "who or what is a Man-Thing." This is Marvel's answer to DC's Swamp Thing, and his wife (Ellen Brandt) was one of the Extremis soldiers working for AIM in Iron Man 3. She and Man-Thing also have ties to Doctor Strange, who was name-dropped in *The Winter Soldier*.

- Coulson mentions The Cube is still functioning. This is the base where Kree supervillain and anti-hero Marvel Boy was held.

- In a series of callbacks to the pilot, Skye takes Ward to the diner where she met Mike Peterson and discusses him in "Nothing Personal" (AS1.20). There's a "superhero jump" from Deathlok. Lola flies once more.

- The drug lord killed by Deathlok in "Ragtag" (AS1.21) may be a nod to El Caiman, a Colombian drug lord from a 1988 comic. Garrett's almost-death scene looks similar to the Extremis effect from *Iron Man 3*.

- In "Ragtag" (AS1.21), the files on Deathlok go all the way back to 1990. He was title character in a four-issue miniseries that debuted in 1990, though the character was invented in a 1974 issue of *Astonishing Tales*.

- Triplett shares a pile of Howling Commandos gear with the team in "Ragtag," (AS1.21). The fake cigarettes, joy buzzers, spy glasses, walkie-talkies and so forth are delightfully retro post-World War II spy gear. "Where did they buy this stuff – in the back of a comic book?" Skye asks. While nodding to comic staples of the past, they foreshadow the tech of *Agent Carter*.

- The Hypno-Beam Triplett produces doesn't appear in Marvel lore but may be a nod to the Hypno-Hustler, an African-American Spider-Man villain from the '70s...his name is Antoine, and thus he's a possible future for Trip.

- May sarcastically says, "Watch out Hydra, here we come," ("Ragtag," AS1.21), the cry of the Invaders.

- Fitz and Simmons are jettisoned in a cell like the Hulk's on *The Avengers*.

- Patton Oswalt plays the Koenig brothers, who may be Life Model Decoys.

- Coulson, May and Triplett use the Asgardian Berserker Staff in "The Beginning of the End" (AS1.22).

- Zeller, the head of the Cybertek facility in "The Beginning of the End" (AS1.22) may be named for Gretchen Zeller, a World War II resistance fighter created by *Captain America: The Winter Soldier* author Ed Brubaker. If he reappears, he may be revealed as her descendent.

- Nick Fury hands Coulson the giant gun from *The Avengers*. In the film, Coulson points the giant firearm at Loki, saying "You like this? We started working on the prototype after you sent the Destroyer. Even I don't know what it does. Do you wanna find out?" The second time, Fury says, "This packs a pretty good punch," and Coulson replies: "I know what it does."

- Coulson was invented in the Marvel Cinematic Universe (beginning with *Iron Man*) as a fan favorite and ordinary man who then appeared in the comics, so it's touching to see Nick Fury appoint him an Avenger.

- At the end of season one, Fury reveals he has a spy eye like the one in "Eye Spy" (AS1.4).

- Clark Gregg voices Coulson on *Ultimate Spider-Man*. The actor notes, "I grew up watching the Spider-Man animated show so when they said, 'Do you want to do Principal Coulson's voice in the Ultimate Spider-Man cartoon?' I was like, 'Yes! Yes, yes, yes, yes. Yes I do! Don't audition anybody, I want to do that.'" (Burlingame).

- Season two emphasizes the Kree and their creation, the Inhumans. Characters steal the obelisk that contained the Terrigen Mist that gives Inhumans their powers, then the device finally activates in the Kree hidden city in the tenth episode.

- "Shadows," (2.1) has a cameo flashback by Peggy Carter and the Howling Commandos. It showed them going after the last Hydra base and meeting Daniel Whitehall (Kraken) and finding the first 0-8-4, the obelisk. The origin of the Kree that provided GH 325 was revealed as well. SSR was introduced. The Red Skull and Howard Stark were also name dropped.

- In "Shadows," (2.1), Coulson shows a map with locations of allies. One in Africa matches Black Panther's home, Wakanda. Other places include Alaska, Canada, 2 in California, a few in England, one in Berlin, 2 in Brazil, one in Paris, one in Alexandria, one in South Africa, one in Egypt, one in Israel, one in Saudi Arabia, one in Moscow, one in the Himalayas. This last might be the Inhumans or the Iron Fist city of Kun Lun. Moonknight could be the light in Egypt, Alpha Flight in Canada. The Westcoast Avengers are based in LA., near Tony Stark.

- Carl "Crusher" Creel, the Absorbing Man" (2.1) also appears in the flashbacks of Daredevil.

- In "Heavy is the Head" (2.2), Raina gives the Absorbing Man a metal that she describes as super strong and coming from the stars – vibranium?

- General Talbot mentions Operation Panther Klaw - Panther's nemesis is the villain Klaw (2.2).

- Tripplet uses the alias General Jones, a nod to Howling Commando Gabe Jones.

- Grant Ward's brother is Senator Christian Ward – Senator Ward is a character introduced in Spider-Man stories who served in the same special forces regiment as Gwen Stacy's father before betraying his team.

- Bobbi Morse, Mockingbird of the comics, is one of the founders of Avengers of the West Coast ("Face My Enemy," 2.4).

- Doctor Faustus is mentioned as the creator of the brainwashing method being used by the Kraken.

- In "The Writing on the Wall" (2.7), Skye gets a tip from "One of my sources, Micro, he's kind of a crime scene junkie." This is "Microchip," David Linus Lieberman from Punisher.

- Skye tells Coulson, "It's all connected. Everything" (2.7) This was a tagline for the MCU's vast sprawl.

- The least crazy of the GH-325 subjects, Hank Thompson, was once "Cameron Klein," a S.H.I.E.L.D. tech from Captain America comics.

- In "The Writing on the Wall" (2.7), Ward mentions that Baron von Strucker is overseas. Strucker was first introduced in the post-credits button of Captain America: The Winter Soldier where he runs a secret Hydra lab and experimented on Quicksilver and Scarlet Witch.

- Lou Ferrigno Jr. plays Agent Hauer in "The Things We Bury" (2.8).

- Agent Carter negotiates with Whitehall in "The Things We Bury" (2.8).

- Mack is taken over by the Kree city. In the comics, the mists sometimes leave people open to suggestion and subserviance, in a parallel for this. The Inhumans have an entire society called Alpha Primitives, their worker drone slave race.

- At the mid-season break, Skye's father reveals himself as Calvin Zabo, "Mr. Hyde," and his daughter as Daisy Johnson, Quake. She is transformed and gains her earthquake powers ("What They Become," 2.10).

- Trip's mother's house has a framed picture from 1944 of the Howling Commandos with Bucky but not Steve Rogers ("Aftershocks," 2.11).

- Lady Sif visits in "Who You Really Are" (2.12). Her adversary, a Kree, tells the team the history of the Kree and Inhumans. Also, Sif smiles at a mention of Thor.

Fitz: Things change, that's what I'm saying, so maybe if you can learn to control this then you could have Avengers level powers. Something like Captain America even.

Simmons: I think it best we keep in mind the unstable nature
of Skye's power. If there is an Avenger equivalent right now,
I'm afraid it's the Hulk.
Fitz: Well, Hulk saved the world last I checked.
"Love in the Time of Hydra" (2.14)

- Skye hides in the cabin built to contain Bruce Banner ("One Door Closes, 2.15).
- Jemma makes inhibitor bracelets that mimic Quake's comic book bracelets.
- "One Door Closes" (2.15) is a second crossover episode with The Winter Soldier, flashing back to a different group of S.H.I.E.L.D. agents during the battle
- Skye becomes an Inhuman and enters their world ("Afterlife, 2.16). The Inhuman "elders" are mentioned. This Chinese-seeming city surrounded by mountains, is likely Attilan, in the comics hidden in a Himalayan Mountain range in China.

Thor: The Dark World

- As Thor and Malekith do battle across the realms, we see several of the Nine Worlds represented. One is a fiery, hell-like dimension which is presumably Muspelheim, the home of Thor's most deadly foe, the Fire Giant Surtur.
- The giant rocky foe Thor smashes to pieces during the opening battle is a Kronan from Saturn, Thor's foes in his first comics appearance. This Kronan is dressed like Korg, a Kronan warrior from the 2006 storyline, Planet Hulk.
- A billboard says "Is Your Journey Really Necessary?" nodding to a billboard in the first film plus the *Journey into Mystery* comic
- Relics appearing as stones are mentioned.
- Loki transforms into Cap, complete with theme song.
- Algrim wears his red and yellow comics helmet.
- The tesseract is described as an infinity stone.

- Loki's "see you in hell" references the Norse dimension Hel.

- Selvig's crazed blackboard notes reference Brane-theory and Schrodinger's Cat, but also notes on the "616 universe"; the Fault, a tear in the fabric of the universe seen in 2009's War of Kings crossover; and the crossroads, a dimension of portals to other dimensions where Doctor Strange once banished the Hulk.

- Stan Lee, a mental patient, wants his shoe back after Selvig's science lecture.

- Post-credits: The Collector shows off his all-important cocoon to the Asgardians. They mention they have the Tesseract, so they want the Collector to have their other Infinity Stone. He says, "One down, five to go."

Captain America: The Winter Soldier

- The Captain America museum exhibit of course features Peggy, Bucky, the Howling Commandos, previous uniforms, and so on.

- The secret S.H.I.E.L.D. base has pictures of Howard Stark and Peggy Carter. Zola takes credit for killing Tony's parents and describes being recruited by S.H.I.E.L.D., as alluded to in *Agent Carter* and *Agents of S.H.I.E.L.D.*

- In *The Ultimates* comic, Steve Rogers's fiancé married Bucky. In the films, Peggy married a soldier whom Cap once saved – there's a chance it might be her friend from *Agent Carter*.

- While Captain America and Falcon are interrogating Jasper Sitwell he mentions one of the men they've been keeping an eye on – Stephen Strange.

Jasper Sitwell: Zola's algorithm is a program...for choosing Insight's targets!
Steve Rogers: What targets?
Jasper Sitwell: You! A TV anchor in Cairo, the Undersecretary of Defense, a high school valedictorian in Iowa city. Bruce

Banner, Stephen Strange, anyone who's a threat to HYDRA! Now, or in the future.

- Black Widow wears a tiny Hawkeye arrow necklace through the film as a nod to her absent partner.

- A mercenary of Cap's archenemy, the Red Skull, and of Hydra, Brock Rumlow (Crossbones) makes his first appearance in *Winter Soldier*. By the end, he's charred to a crisp, with criss-crossed gun straps make as a translation of his comic costume.

- One of the scientists reprogramming Bucky is actually Ed Brubaker, the man who created *The Winter Soldier* comics arc and greatly influenced the film.

- Nick Fury's tombstone reads, "The Path of the Righteous Man, Ezekiel 25:17" which is the same speech Samuel L. Jackson preached in *Pulp Fiction*.

- The S.H.I.E.L.D. ship that features in the opening sequence is called the Lemurian Star. In comic book continuity, Lemuria is a continent taken over by the Deviants, a race of monsters created by the Celestials.

- Stan Lee Cameo: He's a security guard at the Smithsonian.

- Post-credits: Baron von Strucker experiments on Quicksilver and Scarlet Witch from *Avengers 2*.

Guardians of the Galaxy

- The Collector has acquired a Chitauri (*The Avengers*) and a Dark Elf (*Thor: The Dark World*).

- Quill's 12% of a plan echoes Tony Stark's 12% credit offered to Pepper Potts in planning Stark Tower in *The Avengers*.

- An image of the Tesseract appears onscreen when the Collector explains the origins of the Infinity Stones.

- Adam Warlock, eventually the wielder and protector of the Infinity Stones, was scripted with a cameo near the end of the film. This was eventually cut, but his cocoon appears in the Collector's lab, then damaged and empty in the post-credits scene.

- Crime bars on the jailbirds' suit legs list their crimes – Gamora and Rocket have a lot.

Director James Gunn notes: We have just tons of reference to Marvel cosmic throughout the movie, and I'm certain the most Marvel Comics characters ever in one movie....I would imagine times 4 really. I mean, you know if you think about 'The Avengers' there was you know a few S.H.I.E.L.D. agents and then all of The Avengers and then be kinda' done. With us with have almost every little character is named after somebody in the comics, and some of 'em are far stretches from what they were in the comics. But you know we try keep those little things in there for the fans and they can go and they can look 'em up and see who they are in the Marvel Wiki page and stuff like that, but there's a lot of characters in there." (Perry)

- Star-Lord says he escaped from Morag after an encounter with the people of Sakaar. Sakaar is the planet Hulk takes over in the "Planet Hulk" storyline of the comics.

- Knowhere, the Collector's base of operations in the film, is the Guardians' base in the comics.

- Early drafts of the script featured an Iron Man cameo – Iron Man has been a member of the Guardians in the comics.

- When Peter Quill first struts through the ruins of Morag, he sees a humanoid skeleton with a horse skull – a Kymellian.

- Peter's forgotten hookup, still on board his ship, is Bereet, named for a Krylorian film star and techno-artist in the *Incredible Hulk* comics.

- Ronan in the film blends his status as a top ranking military official (616 universe) and an ally of Thanos (the Ultimate comics). The film version combines elements from a few different takes on Ronan, calling him a Kree "fanatic" hellbent on destroying Xandar. In the comics, Ronan is an elite member of the Kree military, bearing the title of "Supreme Accuser" but he does get to hint at his formal title when he informs the people of Xandar that they stand "accused" moments before he attempts to wipe them from existence.

- The prison facility dubbed The Kyln contrasts with the one in the comics, a power plant that also houses inmates.

- The Nova Corps city of Xandar, as well as all of their ships, was designed with an iconic Star Symbol, nodding to future appearances of the Marvel character Nova.

- Rhommann Dey (John C. Reilly) is one of the few remaining Nova Corps members of Xandar who inducted Richard Rider into its ranks in the comics. Another member, Garthan Saal, was driven mad with power and anger after Nebula destroyed the planet's population.

- Thanos always sits on his impressive throne in the comics.

- Ophelia Lovibond's assistant Carina is meant to be Carina Walters, daughter of the Collector, and future wife of Michael Korvac (the villain known as 'The Enemy').

- Kevin Bacon is mentioned throughout the film (along with his movie *Footloose*). Bacon appeared in James Gunn's previous film Super, and also Marvel's *X-Men: First Class*.

- Peter Quill/Star-Lord refers to their group as "a bunch of losers." Zoe Saldana previously starred in a comic book film called The Losers, about alongside Chris Evans.

- In the movie, Yondu (Michael Rooker) is a mercenary. In the comics, he's actually a founding member of the Guardians of the Galaxy.

- As Quill's ship takes off at film's end, three suns appear in a icky Mouse shape. This was the first non-Avengers Marvel property developed by Disney.

- Knowhere is described as being "the head of a celestial being", and Marvel fans noticed this as the introduction of the Celestials, who spur on other planets' evolution.
- While The Collector tells us the history of the Infinity Stones, Eson the Searcher from the Celestials appears.
- Cosmo the dog appears
- Stan Lee chats up an alien babe
- Post Credits: Howard the Duck (The snarky duck previously starred in a problematic Lucas film in 1986.)

Agent Carter

- Howard Stark and his inventions bridge from *Captain America* to *Agent Carter* to the *Iron Man* films. Tony and Howard both are womanizing geniuses who build terrible weapons, which they're horrified by the government appropriating.
- Howard's butler Edwin Jarvis clearly was the model for Tony's AI butler named J.A.R.V.I.S, an acronym for "Just a Rather Very Intelligent System." Both are British and have a dry wit.
- With their British accents and his propriety, Jarvis and Peggy come across as Steed and Peel – possibly a terribly pun as their series back in the 1960s was called *The Avengers.*
- When Peggy Carter needs help tracking down Howard Stark's missing Nitramene, Jarvis takes her to see Anton Vanko, a Soviet scientist who works for Stark Industries. This foreshadows (or the reverse of that) Anton Vanko's appearance in *Iron Man 2.*
- Roxxon Oil, which sponsors the "Captain America Adventure" radio program that infuriates Peggy, loses a refinery in the first episode. The show itself nods to the comics world of the Golden Age as well as the lost superhero.
- When Peggy uses the VitaRay machine to detect it on the Roxxon staff, we see the machine belongs to A.

Erskine. This references Dr. Abraham Erskine, the scientist behind Steve Rogers's transformation into supersoldier Captain America.

- Hugh Jones of the Serpent Society appears.
- Enver Gjokaj (Daniel Sousa) also plays a NYPD officer during *The Avengers'* climactic battle.
- Lucky Star cab company also appears in *Captain America*
- When Peggy visits the Griffith for the first time, her friend Angie gossips about the residents. She mentions in passing a woman named Mary, a legal secretary at "Goodman, Kurtzberg & Holliway." In the *She-Hulk* comics, Jennifer Walters works at the law firm "Goodman, Lieber, Kurtzberg & Holliway," a nod to Marvel legends Martin Goodman, Stan Lee (née Lieber), Jack Kirby (née Kurtzman).
- The name Leet Brannis, which begins as a mystery, is a minor thief character from the 1940s, a nice tie to the Golden Age in the retro series.
- Peggy rejoins the Howling Commandos in "The Iron Curtain."
- Of course, Dottie is an early product of the Black Widow program – more of this will be seen in Natasha's backstory in *Age of Ultron*.
- James Montgomery Falsworth, a Howling Commando in the MCU and Invader in the comics, is known in the comics as Union Jack. Dum-Dum suggests Miss Union Jack as a name for Peggy Carter.
- The heating vest parallels the Iron Man protective suit … though both sometimes explode.
- The power of creating illusions happens when Dr. Ivchenko turns a ring – this may actually be a ring of the Mandarin's – one has this power.
- Carter tries to stop Howard Stark from crashing the plane, much like the *Captain America* scene.

- Carter's pouring out Steve's blood may spark the Hulk and Deathlok programs as the last of the formula is now lost.
- Stan Lee Cameo: In "The Blitzkrieg Button" he gets his shoes shined beside Howard Stark.
- Post-Credits: Dr. Faustus meets Zola at the end.

Daredevil

- The costumes, but also the camera angles and lighting are directly from many iconic *Daredevil* runs. Images grabbed straight from Frank Miller or Bendis/Maleev or even the Kevin Smith run are clear.
- The black costume comes from Frank Miller and John Romita, Jr.'s *Man Without Fear* miniseries as he takes down a human trafficking ring in his early days . When Daredevil dons his classic red suit, it is an adaptation of the costume he wore in *Secret Wars*.
- In the first episode, there are three references to the "incident" in the Avengers that nearly destroyed Hell's Kitchen and led to many renovation projects and new opportunities in the city. The realtor explains of this nickname, "it sounds so much better than 'death and destruction raining from the sky nearly wiping Hell's Kitchen off the map'." "Heroes and their consequences are why we have our current opportunities" Leland says.
- Matt unwinds at Fogwell's Gym, which appears in the first comic as the place where "a story different from any you have ever read before" first began.
- In Matt's gym in the first episode, a sign on the wall references a fight between Carl "Crusher" Creel and Matt's father, which takes place in the second episode. Creel appeared on *Agents of S.H.I.E.L.D.* 2.1 as the Absorbing Man.
- In the first and third episodes Rob Morgan plays Turk Barrett, a small time criminal who first appeared in *Daredevil* vol. 1 #69.

- Claire Temple blends her comic namesake with the character of Night Nurse. In the comic books, Temple is the ex-wife of Bill Foster and a romantic interest of Luke Cage, so she's likely to cross between the series. Her friend she's apartment sitting for may also appear.

- Claire calls Matt "Mike" before she learns his name, nodding to Matt's comics disguise as Mike Murdock, his own twin brother.

- Josie's Bar is from the comics.

- The former owner of Matt and Foggy's offices, Van Lunt Real Estate Co., is owned by supervillain Cornelius Van Lunt, "Taurus." Their neighbor, Atlas Investments, nods to Atlas Comics, Marvel's predecessor.

- Father Lantom is from Marvel Comics, particularly the *Runaways* series.

- Leland Owlsley is the Daredevil comics villain the Owl.

- As Battling Jack considers taking a dive in flashback, a poster nods to production designer Loren Weeks, art director Toni Barton, and the art department's Dennis Moyes and Chan Lin, along with writers Christos and Ruth Gage, Luke Kalteux, and artist Lee Weeks, among others.

- The man telling him to take the dive, called "Roscoe," is Roscoe "The Fixer" Sweeney, the Marvel Comics villain responsible for fixing fights.

- Vanessa jokes about a previous suitor who wore a "white suit and ascot" ("In the Blood," 1.4). She and Fisk decide this is weird, though this has been Kingpin's iconic suit for decades.

- "If he had an iron suit or a magic hammer, maybe that would explain why you keep getting your asses handed to you." Cap also gets a mention, when Foggy remarks, "I could say I'm Captain America but that doesn't put wings on my head" ("In the Blood," 1.4).

- In episode five, "World on Fire," Claire is disappointed that Matt isn't a disguised billionaire, presumably referencing Tony Stark.
- Fisk comments, "The rising tide raises all boats" (1.5). Is this Skye's organization getting a nod?
- Foggy jokes that Karen should be nice to the old computer parts she purchased, "for when the machines take over" (1.5). This may nod to *Age of Ultron*.
- The question mark insignia marking Madame Gao's heroin is the symbol of Iron Fist villain Steel Serpent, introducing that show to come.
- Frank Miller's arc of the multitude of ninjas in Hell's Kitchen serving The Hand is introduced in this season.
- Matt winds up at St. Agnes' Orphanage, where *Agents of S.H.I.E.L.D.*'s Skye ended up for a time ("Stick," 1.7).
- Matt's Mentor Stick (Scott Glenn) is from the comics of course, but also Stick's boss has been reported to be 'Stone,' Stick's pupil in the comics ("Stick," 1.7).
- The Stick describes young Matt Murdock as "Gifted," suggesting he's like a mutant ("Stick," 1.7).
- The shipping container bringing "Black Sky" to shore is labeled (in Japanese) as "Asano Robotics," owned by "Iron Man" villain Yoshida Asano – Samurai Steel ("Stick," 1.7).
- Episode eight, with the revelation about Fisk's father, sees him borrowing from Rigoletto. In the comics, mob boss Don Rigoletto hired Fisk as his enforcer, before Fisk defeated him and took his criminal empire ("Shadows in the Glass").
- Foggy mentions "the Greek girl" Matt liked – Elektra Natchios, presumably ("Nelson v. Murdock." 1.10)
- One of the framed *New York Bulletins* in the background of Ben Urich's office is a cover story on the Battle of New York from *The Avengers* (1.10).
- Episode ten ("Nelson v. Murdock") has Roxxon persecuting a little guy in a legal maneuver.

- Kingpin's tailor, Melvin Potter, designs many costumes in Hell's Kitchen's criminal underworld. His workshop has several notable pieces, including Stilt-Man's signature legs and buzzsaw arms for Potter's future alter-ego, "Gladiator." Potter is also played by Matt Gerald, who previously appeared in the Marvel one-shot *All Hail The King* as "White Power Dave."

- Daredevil's image in the paper when he gets his name is a clear homage to Alex Maleev's cover for *Daredevil* vol. 2, #60 ("Daredevil," 1.13).

- In the last episode, Stan Lee's cameo appears as a portrait on the wall, to the right of their friend the police officer Brett Mahoney ("Daredevil," 1.13).

THE AVENGERS FACE THEIR DARK SIDES

Conclusion

Kevin Feige and his team have done much to shake up their universe since its invention. New York was torn apart by the Chitauri and the people of earth learned superheroes exist. S.H.I.E.L.D. came forth from the shadows, only to be torn down from within. Feige notes that "we wanted Cap and really the entire cinematic universe to be very different at the end of *Winter Soldier* than it is at the beginning. Therefore when we meet the Avengers at the top of *Age of Ultron*, it's a very different landscape than we left them at the end of the last film" (Brew). Now as several characters comb the galaxy for the Infinity Stones that will empower them to rule the universe, earth will be dragged into intergalactic conflict.

The next stage of films and shows are also lined up: After *Ant Man* (2015) are coming *Captain America: Civil War* and *Doctor Strange* in 2016; *Guardians of the Galaxy 2*, *Thor: Ragnarok* and *Black Panther* in 2017; *The Avengers: Infinity War — Part I*, *Captain Marvel* and *Inhumans* in 2018; and *The Avengers: Infinity War — Part II* in 2019.

Agents of S.H.I.E.L.D. is growing strong, after the first season's complete upheaval and destruction of S.H.I.E.L.D. after the events of *Winter Soldier*. It's already introduced the Inhumans. Meanwhile, in a parallel to Marvel's Phase One, *Daredevil* is the first of four planned Marvel Netflix shows, leading directly into *Jessica Jones*, which brings us into the world of Luke Cage, then Danny Rand (Iron Fist) and sets us up for *The Defenders* show. There are tie-in computer games, comics, toys, and products by the Hulkload.

Yet all these stories do more than flash Cap's shield on Tony's workbench or glimpses of Howard the Duck in nods to older Marvel moments. By saving the world, characters manage to rescue and reassemble the missing pieces of themselves, questing for psychological wholeness. And by watching the heroes face their problems and learn to accept them, we the fans can do likewise.

Glossary

Adaptation: The art of transferring a work from one medium to another.

Agent Carter: 2015 television miniseries starring Peggy Carter and the SSR just before S.H.I.E.L.D. is formed.

Agents of S.H.I.E.L.D.: A television show (2013-) in the Marvel Cinematic Universe (MCU) featuring Agent Coulson's team working behind the scenes. Joss Whedon and his brother and sister-in-law are showrunners.

Alternate Universe, Alt-Universe: Genre that changes elements of the source work, such as having Superman raised on Krypton or adopted by different parents on earth. *The Ultimates* are alternate universe.

Anima: A man's inner female

Animus: A woman's inner male

Auteur: The author brand (in this case largely the vision of MCU producer Kevin Feige), not necessarily the same as the actual writer.

Canon: Material designated "official" or "sanctioned by the author" contrasted with other authors' contributions to a franchise (The *Star Wars* movies, for instance, are considered canon; the spin-off novels and comics are not). The comic books and films have separate, often contradictory details, as do movies by other adaptors.

Comic book: A short collection of comic pages published in a magazine format, often serialized.

Cosplay: Short for "costume play." Wearing costumes and occasionally acting them out.

Daredevil: A 2015 Netflix show, more violent than other works in the MCU.

Dark Lord: The destructive tyrant as Patriarch, classic Shadow and antagonist for the male hero

Deconstruction Age: Mid-1980s-1990s. Comics from this time, like *Watchmen* and *Dark Knight Returns* questioned the nature of the superheroes themselves. Frank Miller's *Daredevil* is among them.

Golden Age: Comics produced between 1938 and the late 1940s. The original Human Torch and Captain America date back to this time. These heroes were generally uncomplicated, altruistically fighting the forces of pure evil. Many major conventions of the genre were established in the forties, as earlier comics had mainly been adventures or thrillers.

Good Mother: Endless source of love and caring, vulnerable angelic side of the self

Hero/Heroine/Chosen One: The rule-breaker who changes the world while growing to adulthood and enlightenment, representing the Self

Inner Child: An immature, unloved self desperate for affection and belonging

Marvel: The publisher of *The Avengers, Agents of S.H.I.E.L.D.,* and many other franchises. Stan Lee is likely its most famous creator.

Marvelverse: Anything that takes place in the fictional world of Marvel Comics, including *The Avengers, X-Men, Fantastic Four,* and *Spider-Man.*

Marvel Cinematic Universe (MCU): This refers only to the movie universe of *Iron Man, Thor, The Avengers, Agent Carter, Agents of S.H.I.E.L.D.,* etc., excluding the more extensive comics.

Mentor: Trains the hero or heroine in qualities needed for adulthood

Ordinary World/Conscious World: Everyday life, the "normal world" of work and polite behavior

Other/Outsider: The outcast or monster rejected by society

Patriarchy: The force of authority and conformity, the restrictive father

Persona: One's superficial self presented to others

Self: The total personality, encompassing many archetypes, including those undiscovered

Shadow/Alter-Ego: One's dark side: everything a person buries and refuses to acknowledge in herself

Silver Age: Comics produced in 1956 through the 1970s. Stan Lee's inventions of *The Hulk, Thor, Iron Man, The Avengers, Fantastic Four, The X-Men,* and *Spider-Man,* finishing with Daredevil, number among these. These superheroes were more conflicted and had to balance jobs and messy family relationships with their heroism.

Superhero: An individual with superhuman powers who fights to protect the innocent.

Transmedia: Works that appear across multiple medias, such as comics, online games, and video.

Trickster: The playful rule-breaker and reverser

Twenty-first century comics: These have a tendency towards dystopia and self-reference, aware as they are of the decades that preceded them. *The Ultimates* can be counted among these, along with the MCU world.

Unconscious World/Magical World: The realm of dreams and fantasies below awareness

THE AVENGERS FACE THEIR DARK SIDES

Works Cited

Primary Sources

Films and Television
Agent Carter Season One. ABC. 2015. Television.
Agents of S.H.I.E.L.D.: Season One. ABC. 2013-2014. Television.
Agents of S.H.I.E.L.D.: Season Two. ABC. 2014-2015. Television.
The Avengers. Dir. Joss Whedon. Disney Studios, 2012. DVD.
Captain America: The First Avenger. Dir. Joe Johnston. Disney Studios, 2011. DVD.
Captain America: The Winter Soldier. Dir. Anthony and Joe Russo. Disney Studios, 2014. DVD.
Daredevil. Netflix, 2015. Online.
Guardians of the Galaxy. Dir. James Gunn. Disney Studios, 2014.
The Incredible Hulk. Dir. Louis Leterrier. Disney Studios, 2008. DVD.
Iron Man. Dir. Jon Favreau. Disney Studios, 2008. DVD.
Iron Man 2. Dir. Jon Favreau. Disney Studios, 2010. DVD.
Iron Man 3. Dir. Shane Black. Disney Studios, 2013. DVD.
Thor. Dir. Kenneth Branagh. Disney Studios, 2011. DVD.
Thor: The Dark World. Dir. Alan Taylor. Disney Studios, 2013. DVD.

Comics
Brubaker, Ed., et al. *Captain America Winter Soldier Ultimate Collection.* New York: Marvel Worldwide, 2014.
Denning, John, ed. *Essential Avengers* Vol. 1 (*Avengers* #1-24). 2011.
Gillen, Kieron and Greg Land. *Iron Man: Believe.* New York: Marvel Worldwide, 2014.
Lee, Stan, et al. *Journey Into Mystery* #83 *Essential Thor Vol. 1* New York: Marvel Comics, 2001.
--. *Journey into Mystery* #124, *Journey into Mystery* #125, *Thor* #126. *Essential Thor* Vol. 2. New York: Marvel Universe, 2005.
--. *Tales of Suspense* #39, #40, #53, #57 *Essential Iron Man* Vol. 1. New York: Marvel Universe, 2007.

Lee, Stan and Jack Kirby. *Avengers* #1, #16, #19. *Essential Avengers*. Vol. 1. New York: Marvel Worldwide, 2009.

--. *Tales of Suspense Featuring Iron Man and Captain America* #80. *Captain America: Marvel Masterworks*. New York: Marvel Worldwide, 2009.

Lee, Stan (w) and John Romita Sr (i). *Amazing Spider-Man* #86 (July 1970). *Black Widow: The Sting of the Widow*. Ed. Jennifer Grunwald. New York: Marvel, 2009.

Lee, Stan, N. Korok (w), and Don Heck (i) *Tales of Suspense* #52 (April 1964). *Black Widow: The Sting of the Widow*. Ed. Jennifer Grunwald. New York: Marvel, 2009.

Michelinie, David and Joe Brozowski. "Why Must There Be An Iron Man?" (*Iron Man* #47) March 1981. *The Many Armors of Iron Man*. Ed. John Kaufman. New York: Marvel Comics, 1992.

Millar, Mark and Bryan Hitch. *The Ultimates Vol. 1: Super-Human*. New York: Marvel Comics, 2006.

--. *The Ultimates Vol. 1: Gods and Monsters*. New York: Marvel Comics, 2006.

--. *The Ultimates 2 Vol. 1: Homeland Security*. New York: Marvel Comics, 2006.

--. *The Ultimates 2 Vol. 2: Grand Theft America*. New York: Marvel Comics, 2007.

Miller, Frank and John Romita Sr. *Daredevil: The Man Without Fear*. New York: Marvel Comics, 2002.

Morrell, David and Mitch Breitweiser. *Captain America: The Chosen*. New York: Marvel Comics, 2008

Thomas, Roy and Barry Smith "Apocalypse Then," (*Iron Man* #144). June 1972. *The Many Armors of Iron Man*. Ed. John Kaufman. New York: Marvel Comics, 1992.

Waid, Mark and Leinil Francis Yu. *Indestructible Hulk: Agent of S.H.I.E.L.D.*, New York: Marvel Worldwide, 2014.

Interviews and Secondary Sources

Beaudet, Denyse. "The Monster." Downing 219-225.

Bercovici, Jeff. "*Avengers* Director Joss Whedon on Trying to Be More Like Buffy." *Forbes* 3 May 2012. http://www.forbes.com/sites/jeffbercovici/2012/05/03/ave

ngers-director-joss-whedon-on-trying-to-be-more-like-buffy.

Biedermann, Hans. *Dictionary of Symbolism*. Trans. James Hulbert. USA: Penguin, 1994.

Blum, Matt "Scarlett Johansson on Black Widow's Character Evolution, Solo Movie Chances, and Kicking Ass in The *Winter Soldier*" Geek Dad 3 April 2014. http://geekdad.com/2014/04/scarlett-johansson-black-widow-winter-soldier.

Brew, Simon. "*Avengers 2*, and a Black Widow solo film." *Den of Geek* 13 Feb 2014. http://www.denofgeek.us/movies/avengers/232989/avenger s-2-and-a-black-widow-solo-film.

Brewer, H. Michael. *Who Needs a Superhero*. Grand Rapids, MI: Baker Books, 2004.

Brooks, Brian, "New York Comic-Con: Netflix's *Daredevil* Unveils New Cast Additions, First Images." *Deadline.com* 11 Oct 2014. http://deadline.com/2014/10/daredevil-new-york-comic-con-netflix-rosario-dawson-charlie-cox-849800.

Brown, Jeffrey A. Dangerous Curves: Action Heroines, Gender, Fetishism, and Popular Culture. USA: University of Mississippi, 2011.

Burlingame, Russ. "Clark Gregg Shares Agent Coulson's Secret (And Unimpressive) Stash." *ComicBook.com* 27 Nov 2013. http://comicbook.com/blog/2013/11/27/clark-gregg-shares-agent-coulsons-secret-and-unimpressive-stash.

Campbell, Joseph. *The Hero with a Thousand Faces*. New York: Princeton University Press, 1973.

Chevalier, Jean and Alain Gheerbrant. *A Dictionary of Symbols*. Trans. John Buchanan-Brown. Oxford: Blackwell, 1994.

Cooper, J.C. *An Illustrated Encyclopedia of Traditional Symbols*. London: Thames and Hudson, Ltd., 1978.

Coyne, S. M. Ruh Linder, J. Rasmussen, E. E. Nelson, D. A. and Collier, K. M. "It's a Bird! It's a Plane! It's a Gender Stereotype!: Longitudinal Associations between Superhero Viewing and Gender Stereotyped Play." *Sex Roles* 70 (2014): 416-430.

Darowski, Joseph. "Invisible, Tiny, and Distant: The First Female Superheroes of the Marvel Age of Comics, Carter, Jones, and Batchelor 199-210.

DeBus, David. "The Self is a Moving Target." Downing 53-62.

Downing, Christine. "Sisters and Brothers." Downing, 110-17.

Downing, Christine., ed. *Mirrors of the Self: Archetypal Images that Shape Your Life.* New York: St. Martin's Press, 1991.

Duncan, Randy and Matthew J. Smith. *The Power of Comics: History, Form, and Culture.* New York: Continuum, 2009.

Dunn, George A. "The Stark Madness of Technology." Irwin, Kindle Location 2419-2690.

Edmunds, T. Keith. "Heroines Aplenty, but None My Mother Would Know: Marvel's Lack of an Iconic Superheroine." Carter, Jones, and Batchelor 221-232.

Estés, Clarissa Pinkola. *Women Who Run With the Wolves.* New York: Ballantine Books, 1992.

Faw, Larissa. "Marvel's Five-Year Plan for *The Avengers* to Rescue the Movies." *Forbes* 30 April 2012. http://www.forbes.com/sites/larissafaw/2012/04/30/marvel s-five-year-plan-for-the-avengers-to-rescue-the-movies.

"Feige on Silver Surfer, Iron Man, Hulk" *SuperheroHype* 10 Feb 2007. http://www.superherohype.com/features/92783-feige-on-silver-surfer-iron-man-and-hulk.

Frankel, Valerie Estelle. *From Girl to Goddess: The Heroine's Journey in Myth and Legend.* Jefferson, NC: McFarland and Co., 2012.

--. *Joss Whedon's Names.* USA: LitCrit Press, 2014.

Granshaw, Lisa. "Meet the Inhumans." *BoingBoing* 3 Mar 2015 http://boingboing.net/2015/03/03/meet-the-inhumans.html.

Grossman, Lev, "The Hero Whisperer." *Time* 179:18 (7 May 2012)..

Hagley, A. and Harrison, M. "Fighting the Battles We Never Could: *The Avengers* and Post-September 11 American Political Identities." *Political Science and Politics* 47:0 (2014): 120-124.

Halterman, Jim "Daredevil Preview: 9 Things to Know About Netflix's Kick Ass Marvel Series." *TV Fanatic* 10 April 2015. http://www.tvfanatic.com/2015/04/daredevil-preview-9-things-to-know-about-netflixs-kick-ass-marve.

Henderson, Joseph L. "Ancient Myths and Modern Man." Jung 95-156.

Iaccino, James F. *Jungian Reflections within the Cinema.* Westport, CO: Praeger Publishers, 1998.

Irwin, William, ed. *Superheroes: The Best of Philosophy and Pop Culture.* USA: John Wiley and Sons. 2011. Kindle Edition.

Jaffé, Aniela. "Symbolism in the Visual Arts" Jung 256-322.

Jung, Carl. *Memories, Dreams, Reflections.* Ed. Aniela Jaffe. Trans. Clara Winston. USA: Vintage, 1989.

Jung, Carl, ed. *Man and His Symbols.* New York: Doubleday, 1964.

Keyes, Rob. "Iron Man 3: Guy Pearce's Aldrich Killian, AIM & Extremis Explained." *Screen Rant* 2013. http://screenrant.com/iron-man-3-aim-extremis.

Keyes, Rob. "Set Interview: Chris Evans Talks 'Captain America 2' & Life as a Marvel Hero." *Screenrant* 2014. http://screenrant.com/chris-evans-interview-captain-america-2-set

Kozak, Jim. "Serenity Now!" *In Focus* Aug/Sept 2005. http://web.archive.org/web/20060102103544/http://www.in focusmag.com/05augustseptember/whedonuncut.htm.

Landay, Lori. *Madcaps, Screwballs, and Con Women: The Female Trickster in American Culture.* Pennsylvania: University of Pennsylvania Press, 1998.

Lee, Stan. "Introduction." *Stan Lee Meets the Amazing Spider-Man* by Stan Lee, Joss Whedon, Olivier Coipel and Michael Gaydos. USA: Marvel Comics, 2006. 11-20.

--. *Origins of Marvel Comics.* New York: Fireside, 1974.

--. Son of Origins of Marvel Comics. New York: Fireside, 1975.

Lee, Stan and George Mair. *Excelsior! The Amazing Life of Stan Lee.* New York: Fireside, 2002.

Leterrier, Louis. "IGN Interview." *Comic Vine* 2009. http://www.comicvine.com/hulk/4005-2267/forums/the-incredible-hulk-discussion-thread-23024.

Maja Bajac-Carter; Norma Jones and Bob Batchelor, eds. *Heroines of Comic Books and Literature: Portrayals in Popular Culture.* USA: Rowman and Littlefield 2014.

Mangels, Andy. *Iron Man: Beneath the Armor.* New York: Del Rey, 2008.

Morrison, Grant. *Supergods: What Masked Vigilantes, Miraculous Mutants, and a Sun God from Smallville Can Teach Us About Being Human.* New York: Spiegel & Grau, 2011.

Murray, Chris. Champions of the Oppressed? Superhero Comics, Popular Culture, and Propaganda in America During World War II. USA: Hampton Press, 2011.

-- . "Propaganda: The Pleasures of Persuasion in *Captain America.*" *Critical Approaches to Comics: Theories and Methods,* eds. Matthew J. Smith and Randy Duncan. New York: Routledge 2011. 129-

141.

Norton, Edward. "Edward Norton Talks The Incredible Hulk" *Total Film* 7 Mar 2008 http://www.gamesradar.com/edward-norton-talks-incredible-hulk.

Packer, Sharon. *Superheroes and Superegos: Analyzing the Minds behind the Masks*. Santa Barbara, CA: ABC-Clio, 2010.

Perry, Spencer. "*Guardians of the Galaxy:* From the Set of the Marvel Studios Adaptation." *Superherohype.com* 8 July 2014. http://www.superherohype.com/news/306737-guardians-of-the-galaxy-from-the-set-of-the-marvel-studios-adaptation.

Radish, Christina. "*Daredevil* Executive Producers Explain How Marvel's Darkest Venture yet Was Created." *Collider* 8 April 2015. http://collider.com/daredevil-tv-show-details-steven-deknight.

Reynolds, Richard. *Super Heroes: A Modern Mythology (Studies in Popular Culture)*. Jackson, University Press of Mississippi, 1992.

Ridout, Cefn. "Introduction." *The Many Armors of Iron Man*. Ed. John Kaufman. New York: Marvel Comics, 1992.

Riviére, Joan. "Womanliness as Masquerade." *Formations of Fantasy*. Eds. Victor Burgin, James Donald, and Cora Kaplan. London: Methuen, 1986.

Rogers, Adam. "Joss Whedon on Comic Books, Abusing Language and the Joys of Genre." *Wired* 3 May 2012. http://www.wired.com/underwire/2012/05/joss-whedon/4.

Ryall, Chris and Scott Tipton. *Comic Books 101: The History, Methods, and Madness*. Cincinnati: Impact Books, 2009.

Stein, Murray. "The Devouring Father." Downing 76-79.

Stuller, Jennifer K. Ink-Stained Amazons and Cinematic Warriors: Superwomen in Modern Mythology. USA: I.B. Tauris, 2010.

Vogler, Christopher. *The Writer's Journey*. Studio City, CA: Michael Wiese Productions, 1998.

Von Franz, M.L.. "The Process of Individuation." Jung 157-254.

Weintraub, Steve. "Shane Black and Kevin Feige Talk *Iron Man 3*, Crafting the Mandarin, the Scripting Process, Iron Patriot, the Film's Connection to *The Avengers*." *Collider* 5 Mar 2013. http://collider.com/iron-man-3-kevin-feige-shane-black-interview.

White, Brett. "Marvel Women of the Seventies: Black Widow." *Marvel.com* 7 July 2014 http://marvel.com/news/comics/22816/marvel_women_of

_the_70s_black_widow.
White, Mark D. "Lord Odin Have Mercy: Justice and Punishment in Asgard." Irwin, Kindle Locations 293-470.
Whitmont, Edward E. "Persona: The Mask We Wear for the Game of Living." Downing 14-18.

THE AVENGERS FACE THEIR DARK SIDES

About the Author

Valerie Estelle Frankel is the author of many books on pop culture, including *Doctor Who – The What, Where, and How*, *History, Sherlock: Every Canon Reference You May Have Missed in BBC's Series 1-3*, *Homages and the Highlands: An Outlander Guide*, and *How Game of Thrones Will End*. Many of her books focus on women's roles in fiction, from her heroine's journey guides *From Girl to Goddess* and *Buffy and the Heroine's Journey* to books like *Women in Game of Thrones* and *The Many Faces of Katniss Everdeen*. Once a lecturer at San Jose State University, she's a frequent speaker at conferences. Come explore her research at www.vefrankel.com.

www.ingramcontent.com/pod-product-compliance
Lightning Source LLC
Chambersburg PA
CBHW031511040426
42445CB00009B/177